A

Collection of English Poems

1660–1800

*

A
COLLECTION
OF
ENGLISH POEMS
1660—1800

Selected and Edited by

RONALD S. CRANE
Professor of English, University of Chicago

NEW YORK *and* LONDON
HARPER & BROTHERS PUBLISHERS

PREFACE

This book is designed primarily for the convenience of advanced students of Restoration and eighteenth-century literature in American colleges and universities. Its main purpose is to give such students, many of whom cannot rely upon access to adequately equipped libraries, a selection of representative poems published in England and Scotland between 1660 and 1800 sufficiently generous to enable them to judge the achievement of the age, in all its variety of themes and styles, for themselves.

It is an age about which it is increasingly easy to form sympathetic and properly instructed views. The prejudices of a hundred years, to be sure, die hard; and there are many readers and critics among us to whom the verdict pronounced by Romantics and Victorians upon the "classical" school of the eighteenth century remains even yet the final word. That true poetry is always a direct outpouring of personal feeling; that its values are determined by the nature of the emotion which it expresses, the standard being naturally set by the preferences of the most admired poets in the nineteenth-century tradition; that its distinctive effort is "to bring unthinkable thoughts and unsayable sayings within the range of human minds and ears"; that the essence of its art is not statement but suggestion—these are still for many persons self-evident propositions; and their effect is still to fasten a taint of the unpoetic upon even the greatest productions of an age which by principle eschewed personal confessions, which loved wit and cultivated regularity, precision, and a "satisfying completeness" of form, and which drew the substance of its verse from such— to the nineteenth century—prosaic things as the scorn of Tory for Whig or of wit for pedant and dunce, as the coming of a city shower, or as the optimistic theory of the world.

But it is clear that the tyranny of these presuppositions about the nature of poetry and of the inhibitions of taste which they have tended to encourage is far less complete at the present moment than it was even a few years ago. There have of course always been readers who have found in the poetry of Dryden and Pope and Swift and Prior and Johnson a source of unfailing delight. The difference is that today such admirers of "classical" verse need no longer feel themselves isolated in the midst of a hostile world. No more are they on the defensive; it is not they but the surviving disciples of Wordsworth and Matthew Arnold who are out of harmony with the movement of modern criticism and taste. Of this movement in the English-speaking world the most influential spokesman is beyond question Mr. T. S. Eliot; no one has done more than he to make us aware of the limitations of Romantic and Victorian ideas about poetry or to win a respectful hearing for poets who worked in idioms foreign to nineteenth-century taste. His essay on Dryden, inspired by the excellent and no less enthusiastic appraisal of Mr. Van Doren, is a manifesto of revolt. "To enjoy Dryden means to pass beyond the limitations of the nineteenth century into a new freedom." "Dryden [in *Mac Flecknoe*] continually enhances: he makes his object great, in a way contrary to expectation; and the total effect is due to the transformation of the ridiculous into poetry." "The reproach of the prosaic, levelled at Dryden, rests upon a confusion between the emotions considered to be poetic—which is a matter allowing considerable latitude of fashion—and the *result* of personal emotion in poetry. . . ." "Dryden lacked what his master Jonson possessed, a large and unique view of life; he lacked insight, he lacked profundity. But where Dryden fails to satisfy, the nineteenth century does not satisfy us either; and where that century has condemned him, it is itself condemned. In the next revolution of taste it is possible that poets may turn to the study of Dryden. He remains one of those who have set standards for English verse which it is desperate to ignore." That these statements represent a view which has become increasingly prevalent, and that not alone in academic circles, since 1920, there is ample evidence in the mass of recent critical comment not merely on Dryden but on many of his successors in the same tradition—on Pope, on Swift, on Johnson, on Churchill, on the numerous minor poets of the Georgian era who have been so diligently collected by Mr. David Nichol Smith and Mr. Iolo Williams. Not every one would endorse the late Mr. Strachey's enthusiasm for Pope's *Pastorals*; but there are many readers nowadays who appreciate what he means when he speaks of "the enchantment of the heroic couplet," and who would subscribe unreservedly to his emancipated view of the subject-matter of poetry: "If we look at the facts, where do we find poetry? In the wild fantasies of Aristophanes, in the sordid lusts of Baudelaire, in the gentle trivialities of La Fontaine. . . . There is poetry to be found lurking in the metaphysical system of Epicurus, and in the body of a flea. And so need we be surprised if it invests a game of cards, or a gentleman sneezing at Hampton Court?"

Many of the barriers which once stood in the way of a full enjoyment of eighteenth-century poetry have thus been broken down—thanks to the critical revolution of the past decade. But this is not all. Appreciation of the verse contained in this volume is dependent upon other things besides an open mind toward forms of poetry not approved by the nineteenth-century tradition; it demands an adequate conception of the culture, the ruling ideas, and in general the artistic and intellectual history of the age in which it was produced. We stand at present only upon the threshold of a proper understanding of the seventeenth and eighteenth centuries; but progress toward such an understanding has been notably rapid during the last few years, and the student who approaches the period today can do so with the help of much more trustworthy and stimulating guides than would have been available a decade ago.[1] It is not merely that we have for the first time satisfactory texts of a number of important poets (Blake, for example), or that the lives and personalities of others (for instance, Pope) have been put in a fairer light, or that diligent inquiry has told us more than we ever knew before about such topics as the origins of the heroic couplet, the vogue of burlesque and mock-heroic poetry, or the influence of Spenser and Milton on eighteenth-century style. Along with much accumulation of new detail and much fruitful sifting of the old there have come also altered perspectives, and a fresh insight into the complex forces that shaped the period as a whole. In this progress the chief factor has undoubtedly been the renewed concentration by scholars on the relations between eighteenth-century literature and the history of ideas. How vivifying the effect of this form of study can be appears most conspicuously perhaps in the scattered writings of Professor Lovejoy.[2] If we are now beginning to have something like an adequate understanding of the intellectual atmosphere surrounding neo-classical criticism and poetry, if we are on our way toward a more discriminating and genuinely historical conception of the complex of movements which has been commonly called "romanticism," the credit must in very large measure go to him. Others at the same time, but independently, have applied a similar method to more limited problems, with results that are no less illuminating in their way. Thus—to mention only a few examples—a good deal that was formerly obscure in Dryden's religious poems has now been cleared up; many aspects of Thomson have acquired new meaning by being brought into relation with the scientific and religious ideas of his time; Blake no longer stands an isolated and hence unintelligible figure in the later eighteenth century.

In selecting and reprinting the poems which make up this volume I have tried to keep in mind both of these new directions of interest in the verse of the period. I have naturally devoted most space to major figures, such as Dryden, Prior, Swift, Gay, Pope, Thomson, Johnson, Collins, Gray, Goldsmith, Cowper, Blake, and Burns; but I have not neglected their lesser contemporaries, many of whom have left us verse of indubitable excellence in forms or on subjects that would have been inadequately illustrated in a selection

[1] The titles of the most important or useful of these are brought together in the bibliography at the end of the volume.

[2] For a list of his principal papers on eighteenth-century topics see the third and fourth sections of the bibliography.

only from the better-known men. With rare exceptions I have included only complete poems or complete parts of poems, and I have taken the texts of these, whenever possible, from the most authoritative contemporary sources, and have printed them unaltered except for the correction of an occasional misprint or the insertion of an occasional needed mark of punctuation.[3] In arranging them in the volume I have followed an order determined, for the whole work of an author, by the date of his first important publication,[4] and, for the individual poems of an author, by the dates, so far as these could be ascertained, of their first appearance in print.[5]

I suppose that no one who undertakes such a work as this can ever feel entirely happy about the printed result. I have omitted some poems which, could I now plan the collection anew, I should certainly wish to include, and I have given valuable space to others of whose superior claims I am no longer quite convinced. In preparing the texts I have not always, as Johnson confessed on a more momentous occasion, "executed my own scheme, or satisfied my own expectations." The difficulties have been greater than I could anticipate. It has not always been easy, and occasionally it has proved impossible, to determine with certainty what particular form of a poem best represented its author's final intentions. I have been reasonably diligent in my inquiries, but so imperfect still is our knowledge of the textual history of this period that I have been forced, more frequently than I could wish, to content myself with what I feel sure are only approximations. Nor, even when I knew what text I ought to print, has it invariably been possible to act upon the information. Certain poems I have been compelled to reproduce from obviously inferior sources; of a number of others I have been obliged to give texts which, though they have been collated in proof with the proper originals, still retain some of the variations in capitalization and punctuation, though not in wording, characteristic of the modern editions from which they were set.[6] And finally I shall not be surprised to learn, though here again I have taken some pains, that the dates of first publication given in the notes are in some instances incorrect. I can only hope that errors of this sort are not unduly numerous and that users of the collection will have the kindness to inform me of any that they may discover.

[3] The source of the text of each poem is indicated in a footnote, though not always, I am afraid, with all the precision that might be demanded in a work of greater scholarly pretensions. It has seemed unnecessary, for example, to take account of the fact that there were duplicate printings, with some textual variations of minor importance, of Cowley's *Works* of 1668, of Prior's *Poems* of 1718, of the *Gentleman's Magazine* for July, 1731, and possibly of others among the editions which I have used.

[4] This appears as the second of the three dates given in parentheses after the name of the author.

[5] To this latter rule I have admitted a few exceptions. Thus poems printed posthumously have normally been placed according to dates of composition.

[6] These poems are designated in the bibliographical footnotes by the phrase "See Preface."

The debt which this book owes to earlier attempts in the same kind, and especially to the admirable anthologies of Iolo Williams and David Nichol Smith, will be evident to all readers. I have received much kind assistance, at various stages in its preparation, from friends both in this country and England. Messrs. Birrell and Garnett, of London, and Mr. Walter Hill, of Chicago, have generously allowed me to collate certain rare books in their possession. Mr. L. F. Powell, the learned and benevolent librarian of the Taylor Institution, Oxford, Professor F. B. Snyder, of Northwestern University, and Professors Sir William Craigie, George L. Marsh, and George Sherburn, of the University of Chicago, have aided me in the choice and verification of the texts and in the preparation of the appendixes. I am under obligation also to Mr. Geoffrey Keynes and the Nonesuch Press for permission to use the text of Blake contained in the excellent one-volume edition of his poetry and prose published in 1927; to the Cambridge University Press for authorization to include the text of Prior's *Jinny the Just* first printed from manuscript by A. R. Waller in 1907; and to the University of Chicago Press for permission to imitate the cover design of my *New Essays by Oliver Goldsmith*. My chief debt, however, is to my assistant, Mr. W. K. Chandler, from whose advice and criticism, freely given during the whole course of the undertaking, I have profited more than I can adequately say.

CONTENTS

xi

A

Collection of English Poems

1660–1800

Abraham Cowley

(1618-1633-1667)

To Sir William Davenant
Upon His Two First Books of Gondibert, Finished
Before His Voyage to America[1]

METHINKS *Heroick Poesie* till now
Like some fantastick *Fairy Land* did show,
Gods, Devils, Nymphs, Witches and *Gyants race,*
And all but *Man* in *Mans chief work* had place.
Thou like some worthy *Knight* with sacred Arms   5
Dost drive the *Monsters* thence, and end the *Charms.*
Instead of those dost *Men* and *Manners* plant,
The things which that rich *Soil* did chiefly want.
Yet ev'en thy *Mortals* do their *Gods* excell,
Taught by thy *Muse* to *Fight* and *Love* so well.   10
   By fatal hands whilst *present Empires* fall,
Thine from the Grave *past Monarchies* recall.
So much more thanks from humane kind does merit
The *Poets Fury,* then the *Zelots Spirit.*
And from the *Grave* thou mak'est this *Empire* rise,   15
Not like some dreadful *Ghost* t'affright our Eyes,
But with more Lustre and triumphant state,
Then when it *crown'd* at proud *Verona* sate.
So will our *God rebuild* mans perisht frame,
And raise him up much *Better,* yet the *same.*   20
So *God-like Poets* do past things reherse,
Not *change,* but *Heighten* Nature by their Verse.
   With shame, methinks, great *Italy* must see
Her *Conqu'erors* rais'd to *Life* again by *Thee.*
Rais'd by such pow'erful Verse, that ancient *Rome*   25
May blush no less to see her *Wit o'ercome.*
Some men their *Fancies* like their *Faith* derive,
And think all Ill but that which *Rome* does give.
The Marks of *Old* and *Catholick* would find,
To the same *Chair* would *Truth* and *Fiction* bind.   30
Thou in those beaten pathes disdain'st to tred,
And scorn'st to *Live* by robbing of the *Dead.*
Since Time does all things change, thou think'st not fit

---

[1] Published in *The Preface to Gondibert,* Paris, 1650. Text of *Works,* 1668.

I

This latter *Age* should see *all New but Wit*.
Thy *Fancy* like a *Flame* its way does make,   35
And leave bright *Tracks* for following Pens to take.
Sure 'twas this noble boldness of the *Muse*
Did thy desire to seek new *Worlds* infuse,
And ne're did Heav'n so much a *Voyage* bless,
If thou canst *Plant* but *there* with like success.   40

Ode. Of Wit[1]

TELL me, O tell, what kind of thing is *Wit*,
    Thou who *Master* art of it.
For the *First matter* loves *Variety* less;
Less *Women* lov't, either in *Love* or *Dress*.
    A thousand different shapes it bears,   5
    Comely in thousand shapes appears.
Yonder we saw it plain; and here 'tis now,
Like *Spirits* in a *Place*, we know not *How*.

London that vents of *false Ware* so much store,
    In no *Ware* deceives us more.   10
For men led by the *Colour*, and the *Shape*,
Like *Zeuxes Birds* fly to the painted *Grape*;
    Some things do through our Judgment pass
    As through a *Multiplying Glass*.
And sometimes, if the *Object* be too far,   15
We take a *Falling Meteor* for a *Star*.

Hence 'tis a *Wit* that greatest *word* of *Fame*
    Grows such a common Name.
And *Wits* by our *Creation* they become,
Just so, as *Tit'lar Bishops* made at *Rome*.   20
    'Tis not a *Tale*, 'tis not a *Jest*
    Admir'd with *Laughter* at a feast,
Nor florid *Talk* which can that *Title* gain;
The *Proofs* of *Wit* for ever must remain.

'Tis not to force some lifeless *Verses* meet   25
    With their five gowty feet.
All ev'ry where, like *Mans*, must be the *Soul*,
And *Reason* the *Inferior Powers* controul.
    Such were the *Numbers* which could call
    The *Stones* into the *Theban* wall.   30

---

[1] Published in *Poems*, 1656. Text of *Works*, 1668.

Such *Miracles* are ceast; and now we see
No *Towns* or *Houses* rais'd by *Poetrie*.

Yet 'tis not to adorn, and gild each part;
   That shows more *Cost,* then *Art.*
Jewels at *Nose* and *Lips* but ill appear;   35
Rather then *all things Wit,* let *none* be there.
   Several *Lights* will not be seen,
   If there be nothing else between.
Men doubt, because they stand so thick i' th' skie,
If those be *Stars* which paint the *Galaxie.*   40

'Tis not when two like words make up one noise;
   Jests for *Dutch Men,* and *English Boys.*
In which who finds out *Wit,* the same may see
In *An'grams* and *Acrostiques Poetrie.*
   Much less can that have any place   45
   At which a *Virgin* hides her face,
Such *Dross* the *Fire* must purge away; 'tis just
The *Author blush,* there where the *Reader* must.

'Tis not such *Lines* as almost crack the *Stage*
   When *Bajazet* begins to rage.   50
Nor a tall *Meta'phor* in the *Bombast way,*
Nor the dry chips of short lung'd *Seneca.*
   Nor upon all things to obtrude,
   And force some odd *Similitude.*
What is it then, which like the *Power Divine*   55
We only can by *Negatives* define?

In a true piece of *Wit* all things must be,
   Yet all things there *agree.*
As in the *Ark,* joyn'd without force or strife,
All *Creatures* dwelt; all *Creatures* that had *Life.*   60
   Or as the *Primitive Forms* of all
   (If we compare great things with small)
Which without *Discord* or *Confusion* lie,
In that strange *Mirror* of the *Deitie.*

But *Love* that moulds *One Man* up out of *Two,*   65
   Makes me forget and injure you.
I took *you* for *my self* sure when I thought
That you in any thing were to be *Taught.*
   Correct my error with thy Pen;
   And if any ask me then,   70
What thing right *Wit,* and height of *Genius* is,
I'll onely shew your *Lines,* and say, *'Tis This.*

The Chronicle. A Ballad[1]

MARGARITA first possesst,
  If I remember well, my brest,
  Margarita first of all;
But when a while the wanton Maid
With my restless Heart had plaid,   5
  Martha took the flying Ball.

Martha soon did it resign
  To the beauteous *Catharine.*
  Beauteous *Catharine* gave place
(Though loth and angry she to part   10
With the possession of my Heart)
  To *Elisa*'s conqu'ering face.

Elisa till this Hour might reign
  Had she not *Evil Counsels* ta'ne.
  Fundamental Laws she broke,   15
And still new *Favorites* she chose,
Till up in *Arms* my *Passions* rose,
  And cast away her yoke.

Mary then and gentle *Ann*
  Both to reign at once began.   20
  Alternately they sway'd,
And sometimes *Mary* was the *Fair*,
And sometimes *Ann* the *Crown* did wear,
  And sometimes *Both* I' obey'd.

Another *Mary* then arose   25
  And did rigorous Laws impose.
  A mighty *Tyrant* she!
Long, alas, should I have been
Under that *Iron-Scepter'd Queen*,
  Had not *Rebecca* set me free.   30

When fair *Rebecca* set me free,
  'Twas then a *golden Time* with me.
  But soon those pleasures fled,
For the gracious Princess dy'd
In her Youth and Beauties pride,   35
  And *Judith* reigned in her sted.

---

[1] Published in *Poems*, 1656. Text of *Works*, 1668.

One Month, three Days, and half an Hour
  Judith held the *Soveraign Power.*
  Wondrous beautiful her Face,
But so weak and small her Wit,   40
That she to govern was unfit,
  And so *Susanna* took her place.

But when *Isabella* came
  Arm'd with a resistless flame
  And th' Artillery of her Eye;   45
Whilst she proudly marcht about
Greater Conquests to find out,
  She beat out *Susan* by the By.

But in her place I then obey'd
  Black-ey'd *Besse,* her *Viceroy-Maid,*   50
  To whom ensu'd a *Vacancy.*
Thousand worse *Passions* then possest
The *Interregnum* of my brest.
  Bless me from such an *Anarchy*!

Gentle *Henriette* than   55
  And a third *Mary* next began,
  Then *Jone,* and *Jane* and *Audria.*
And then a pretty *Thomasine,*
And then another *Katharine,*
  And then a *long Et cætera.*   60

But should I now to you relate,
  The strength and riches of their *state,*
  The *Powder, Patches,* and the *Pins,*
The *Ribbans, Jewels,* and the *Rings,*
The *Lace,* the *Paint,* and *warlike things*   65
  That make up all their *Magazins*:

If I should tell the politick Arts
  To take and keep mens hearts,
  The Letters, Embassies, and Spies,
The Frowns, and Smiles, and Flatteries,   70
The Quarrels, Tears, and Perjuries,
  Numberless, *Nameless Mysteries*!

And all the *Little Lime-twigs* laid
  By *Matchavil* the *Waiting-Maid*;
  I more voluminous should grow   75
(Chiefly if I like them should tell
All Change of *Weathers* that befell)
  Then *Holinshead* or *Stow.*

But I will briefer with them be,
  Since few of them were long with Me.   80
An higher and a nobler strain
My present *Empress* does claim,
Heleonora, First o'th' Name;
  Whom *God grant long to reign!*

Anacreontiques: or, Some Copies of Verses Translated Paraphrastically out of Anacreon[1]

Drinking

THE thirsty *Earth* soaks up the *Rain*,
And drinks, and gapes for drink again.
The *Plants* suck in the *Earth*, and are
With constant drinking fresh and fair.
The *Sea* it self, which one would think   5
Should have but little need of *Drink*,
Drinks ten thousand *Rivers* up,
So fill'd that they or'eflow the *Cup*.
The busie *Sun* (and one would guess
By's drunken fiery face no less)   10
Drinks up the *Sea*, and when h'as done,
The *Moon* and *Stars* drink up the *Sun*.
They drink and dance by their own light,
They drink and revel all the night.
Nothing in *Nature's Sober* found,   15
But an eternal *Health* goes round.
Fill up the *Bowl* then, fill it high,
Fill all the *Glasses* there, for why
Should every creature drink but *I*,
Why, *Man* of *Morals*, tell me why?   20

The Praise of Pindar. In Imitation of Horace his second Ode, B. 4. Pindarum quisquis studet æmulari, &c.[2]

PINDAR is imitable by none;
The *Phœnix Pindar* is a vast *Species alone.*
Who e're but *Dædalus* with waxen wings could fly
And neither *sink* too low, nor *soar* too high?

---

[1] Published in *Poems*, 1656. Text of *Works*, 1668.
[2] Published in *Poems*, 1656. Text of *Works*, 1668.

What could he who *follow'd* claim,   5
But of vain *boldness* the unhappy fame,
    And by his fall a *Sea* to name?
    Pindars unnavigable Song
Like a swoln *Flood* from some steep *Mountain* pours along.
    The *Ocean* meets with such a *Voice*   10
From his enlarged *Mouth,* as drowns the *Oceans* noise.

So *Pindar* does new *Words* and *Figures* roul
Down his impetuous *Dithyrambique Tide,*
    Which in no *Channel* deigns t'abide,
    Which neither *Banks* nor *Dikes* controul.   15
    Whether th' *Immortal Gods* he sings
    In a no less *Immortal strain,*
Or the great Acts of *God-descended Kings,*
Who in his Numbers still survive and *Reign.*
    Each rich embroidered *Line,*   20
    Which their triumphant *Brows* around,
    By his sacred Hand is bound,
Does all their *starry Diadems* outshine.

Whether at *Pisa*'s race he please
To *carve* in polisht *Verse* the *Conque'rors Images,*   25
Whether the *Swift,* the *Skilful,* or the *Strong,*
Be crowned in his *Nimble, Artful, Vigorous* Song:
Whether some brave young mans untimely fate
In words worth *Dying for* he celebrate,
    Such *mournful,* and such *pleasing* words,   30
As *joy* to his *Mothers* and his *Mistress grief* affords:
    He bids him *Live* and *Grow* in fame,
    Among the *Stars* he sticks his *Name:*
The *Grave* can but the *Dross* of him devour,
So *small* is *Deaths,* so *great* the *Poets* power.   35

Lo, how th'obsequious *Wind,* and swelling *Ayr*
    The *Theban Swan* does upwards bear
Into the *walks* of *Clouds,* where he does play,
And with extended *Wings* opens his liquid way.
    Whilst, alas, my *tim'erous Muse*   40
    Unambitious tracks pursues;
    Does with weak unballast wings,
    About the *mossy Brooks* and *Springs;*
    About the *Trees* new-blossom'ed *Heads,*
    About the *Gardens* painted *Beds,*   45
    About the *Fields* and flowry *Meads,*

And all *inferior beauteous things*
  Like the laborious *Bee*,
For little drops of *Honey* flee,
And there with *Humble Sweets* contents her *Industrie.*   50

To the Royal Society[1]

PHILOSOPHY the great and only Heir
  Of all that Human Knowledge which has bin
Unforfeited by Mans rebellious Sin,
    Though full of years He do appear,
(Philosophy, I say, and call it, He,   5
For whatsoe'er the Painters Fancy be,
    It a Male-virtue seems to me)
Has still been kept in Nonage till of late,
Nor manag'd or enjoy'd his vast Estate:
Three or four thousand years one would have thought,   10
To ripeness and perfection might have brought
  A Science so well bred and nurst,
And of such hopeful parts too at the first.
But, oh, the Guardians and the Tutors then,
(Some negligent, and some ambitious men)   15
    Would ne're consent to set him Free,
Or his own Natural Powers to let him see,
Lest that should put an end to their Autoritie.

That his own business he might quite forget,
They' amus'd him with the sports of wanton Wit,   20
With the Desserts of Poetry they fed him,
In stead of solid meats t' encrease his force;
In stead of vigorous exercise they led him
Into the pleasant Labyrinths of ever-fresh Discourse:
  In stead of carrying him to see   25
The Riches which doe hoorded for him lie
  In Natures endless Treasurie,
  They chose his Eye to entertain
  (His curious but not covetous Eye)
With painted Scenes, and Pageants of the Brain.   30
Some few exalted Spirits this latter Age has shown,
That labour'd to assert the Liberty
(From Guardians, who were now Usurpers grown)
Of this old *Minor* still, Captiv'd Philosophy;
  But 'twas Rebellion call'd to fight   35
  For such a long-oppressed Right.

---

[1] Published in Sprat's *History of the Royal Society*, 1667. Text of *Works*, 1668.

Bacon at last, a mighty Man, arose
  Whom a wise King and Nature chose
  Lord Chancellour of both their Lawes,
And boldly undertook the injur'd Pupils cause.   40

Autority, which did a Body boast,
Though 'twas but Air condens'd, and stalk'd about,
Like some old Giants more Gigantic Ghost,
  To terrifie the Learned Rout
With the plain Magick of true Reasons Light,   45
  He chac'd out of our sight,
Nor suffer'd Living *Men* to be misled
  By the vain shadows of the Dead:
To Graves, from whence it rose, the conquer'd Phantome fled;
  He broke that Monstrous God which stood   50
In midst of th' Orchard, and the whole did claim,
  Which with a useless Sith of Wood,
  And something else not worth a name,
  (Both vast for shew, yet neither fit
  Or to Defend, or to Beget;   55
  Ridiculous and senceless Terrors!) made
Children and superstitious Men afraid.
  The Orchard's open now, and free;
Bacon has broke that Scare-crow Deitie;
  Come, enter, all that will,   60
Behold the rip'ned Fruit, come gather now your Fill.
  Yet still, methinks, we fain would be
  Catching at the Forbidden Tree,
  We would be like the Deitie,
When Truth and Falshood, Good and Evil, we   65
Without the Sences aid within our selves would see;
  For 'tis God only who can find
  All Nature in his Mind.

From Words, which are but Pictures of the Thought,
(Though we our Thoughts from them perversly drew)   70
To things, the Minds right Object, he it brought,
Like foolish Birds to painted Grapes we flew;
He sought and gather'd for our use the True;
And when on heaps the chosen Bunches lay,
He prest them wisely the Mechanick way,   75
Till all their juyce did in one Vessel joyn,
Ferment into a Nourishment Divine,
  The thirsty Souls refreshing Wine.
Who to the life an exact Piece would make,
Must not from others Work a Copy take;   80
  No, not from *Rubens* or *Vandike*;
  Much less content himself to make it like

Th' Idæas and the Images which lie
In his own Fancy, or his Memory.
   No, he before his sight must place   85
   The Natural and Living Face;
   The real object must command
Each Judgment of his Eye, and Motion of his Hand.

From these and all long Errors of the way,
In which our wandring Prædecessors went,   90
And like th' old *Hebrews* many years did stray
   In Desarts but of small extent,
Bacon, like *Moses*, led us forth at last,
   The barren Wilderness he past,
   Did on the very Border stand   95
   Of the blest promis'd Land,
And from the Mountains Top of his Exalted Wit,
   Saw it himself, and shew'd us it.
But Life did never to one Man allow
Time to Discover Worlds, and Conquer too;   100
Nor can so short a Line sufficient be
To fadome the vast depths of Natures Sea:
   The work he did we ought t' admire,
And were unjust, if we should more require
From his few years, divided 'twixt th' Excess   105
Of low Affliction, and high Happiness.
For who on things remote can fix his sight,
That's always in a Triumph, or a Fight?

From you, great Champions, we expect to get
These spacious Countries but discover'd yet;   110
Countries where yet in stead of Nature, we
Her Images and Idols worship'd see:
These large and wealthy Regions to subdue,
Though Learning has whole Armies at command,
   Quarter'd about in every Land,   115
A better Troop she ne're together drew.
   Methinks, like *Gideon*'s little Band,
   God with Design has pickt out you,
To do these noble Wonders by a Few:
When the whole Host he saw, They are (said he)   120
   Too many to o'rcome for Me;
   And now he chuses out his Men,
   Much in the way that he did then;
   Not those many whom he found
   Idely extended on the ground,   125
   To drink with their dejected head

The Stream just so as by their Mouths it fled:
   No, but those Few who took the waters up,
And made of their laborious Hands the Cup.

Thus you prepar'd; and in the glorious Fight   130
   Their wondrous pattern too you take:
Their old and empty Pitchers first they brake,
And with their Hands then lifted up the Light.
   Io! Sound too the Trumpets here!
Already your victorious Lights appear;   135
New Scenes of Heaven already we espy,
And Crowds of golden Worlds on high;
Which from the spacious Plains of Earth and Sea;
   Could never yet discover'd be
By Sailers or *Chaldæans* watchful Eye.   140
Natures great Workes no distance can obscure,
No smalness her near Objects can secure;
   Y' have taught the curious Sight to press
   Into the privatest recess
Of her imperceptible Littleness.   145
   Y' have learn'd to Read her smallest Hand,
And well begun her deepest Sense to Understand.

Mischief and true Dishonour fall on those
Who would to laughter or to scorn expose
So Virtuous and so Noble a Design,   150
So Human for its Use, for Knowledge so Divine.
The things which these proud men despise, and call
   Impertinent, and vain, and small,
Those smallest things of Nature let me know,
Rather than all their greatest Actions Doe.   155
Whoever would Deposed Truth advance
   Into the Throne usurp'd from it,
Must feel at first the Blows of Ignorance,
   And the sharp Points of Envious Wit.
So when by various turns of the Celestial Dance,   160
   In many thousand years
   A Star, so long unknown, appears,
Though Heaven it self more beauteous by it grow,
It troubles and alarms the World below,
Does to the Wise a Star, to Fools a Meteor show.   165

With Courage and Success you the bold work begin;
   Your Cradle has not Idle bin:
None e're but *Hercules* and you could be
At five years Age worthy a History.
   And ne're did Fortune better yet   170

Th' Historian to the Story fit:
    As you from all Old Errors free
And purge the Body of Philosophy;
    So from all Modern Follies He
Has vindicated Eloquence and Wit.   175
His candid Stile like a clean Stream does slide,
    And his bright Fancy all the way
    Does like the Sun-shine in it play;
It does like *Thames*, the best of Rivers, glide,
Where the God does not rudely overturn,   180
    But gently pour the Crystal Urn,
And with judicious hand does the whole Current Guide.
'T has all the Beauties Nature can impart,
And all the comely Dress without the paint of Art.

Sir William Davenant

(1606-1635-1668)

Gondibert, An Heroick Poem[1]

Book II, Canto V

The House of Astragon; *where in distress*
Of Nature, Gondibert *for Art's redress*
Was by old Ulfin *brought: where Art's hard strife,*
In studying Nature for the aid of Life,
Is by full wealth and conduct easie made;
And Truth much visited, though in her shade.

From *Brescia* swiftly o're the bord'ring Plain,
    Return we to the House of *Astragon*;
Where *Gondibert*, and his successful Train,
    Kindly lament the Victory they won.

But though I Fame's great Book shall open now,   5
    Expect a while, till she that *Decad* reads,
Which does this Dukes eternal Story show,
    And aged *Ulfin* cites for special deeds.

Where Friendship is renown'd in *Ulfinore*;
    Where th' ancient musick of delightful verse,   10

---

[1] Published in 1650. Text of *Works*, 1673.

Does it no less in *Goltho's* Breast adore,
    And th' union of their equal hearts reherse.

These weary Victors the descending Sun
    Led hither, where swift Night did them surprise;
And where, for valiant toiles, wise *Astragon*,   15
    With sweet rewards of sleep, did fill their Eyes.

When to the needy World Day did appear,
    And freely op'd her Treasury of light,
His House (where Art and Nature Tennants were)
    The pleasure grew, and bus'ness of their sight.   20

Where *Ulfin* (who an old Domestick seems,
    And rules as Master in the Owners Breast)
Leads *Goltho* to admire what he esteems;
    And thus, what he had long observ'd, exprest.

Here Art by such a diligence is serv'd,   25
    As does th' unwearied Planets imitate;
Whose motion (life of Nature) has preserv'd
    The world, which God vouchsaf'd but to create.

Those heights, which else Dwarf Life could never reach,
    Here, by the wings of diligence they climbe;   30
Truth (skar'd with Terms from canting Schools) they teach;
    And buy it with their best sav'd Treasure, Time,

Here all Men seem Recov'rers of time past;
    As busie as intentive *Emmets* are;
As alarm'd Armies that intrench in haste,   35
    Or Cities, whom unlook'd-for sieges skare.

Much it delights the wise Observers Eye,
    That all these toiles direct to sev'ral skills;
Some from the Mine to the hot Furnace hie,
    And some from flowry Fields to weeping Stills.   40

The first to hopefull *Chymicks* matter bring,
    Where Med'cine they extract for instant cure;
These bear the sweeter burthens of the Spring;
    Whose vertues (longer known) though slow, are sure.

See there wet *Divers* from *Fossone* sent!   45
    Who of the Seas deep Dwellers knowledge give;
Which (more unquiet then their Element)
    By hungry war, upon each other live.

Pearl to their Lord, and Cordial Coral these
   Present; which must in sharpest liquids melt;   50
He with *Nigella* cures that dull disease
   They get, who long with stupid Fish have dwelt.

Others through Quarries dig, deeply below
   Where Desart Rivers, cold, and private run;
Where Bodies conservation best they know,   55
   And Mines long growth, and how their veines begun.

He shewes them now Tow'rs of prodigious height,
   Where Natures Friends, Philosophers remain
To censure Meteors in their cause and flight,
   And watch the Wind's authority on Rain.   60

Others with Optick Tubes the Moons scant face
   (Vaste Tubes, which like long Cedars mounted lie)
Attract through Glasses to so near a space,
   As if they came not to survey, but prie.

Nine hasty Centuries are now fulfill'd,   65
   Since Opticks first were known to *Astragon*;
By whom the Moderns are become so skill'd,
   They dream of seeing to the Maker's Throne.

And wisely *Astragon*, thus busie grew,
   To seek the Stars remote societies;   70
And judge the walks of th' old, by finding new;
   For Nature's law, in correspondence lies.

Man's pride (grown to Religion) he abates,
   By moving our lov'd Earth; which we think fix'd;
Think all to it, and it to none relates;   75
   With others motion scorn to have it mix'd;

As if 'twere great and stately to stand still
   Whilst other Orbes dance on; or else think all
Those vaste bright Globes (to shew God's needless skill)
   Were made but to attend our little Ball.   80

Now near a sever'd Building they discern'd
   (Which seem'd, as in a pleasant shade, retir'd)
A Throng, by whose glad diligence they learn'd,
   They came from Toyles which their own choice desir'd.

This they approach, and as they enter it   85
   Their Eyes were stay'd, by reading o'er the Gate,

GREAT NATURES OFFICE, in large letters writ;
　　And next, they mark'd who there in office sate.

Old busie Men, yet much for wisdom fam'd;
　　Hasty to know, though not by haste beguil'd;   90
These fitly, NATURE'S REGISTERS were nam'd;
　　The Throng were their INTELLIGENCERS stil'd:

Who stop by snares, and by their chace o'retake
　　All hidden Beasts the closer Forrest yields;
All that by secret sence their rescue make,   95
　　Or trust their force, or swiftness in the Fields.

And of this Throng, some their imployment have
　　In fleeting Rivers, some fix'd Lakes beset;
Where Nature's self, by shifts, can nothing save
　　From trifling Angles, or the swal'wing Net.   100

Some, in the spacious Ayre, their Prey o'retake,
　　Cous'ning, with hunger, Falcons of their wings;
Whilst all their patient observations make,
　　Which each to NATURE'S OFFICE duely brings.

And there of ev'ry Fish, and Foule, and Beast,   105
　　The wiles these learned *Registers* record,
Courage, and feares, their motion and their rest;
　　Which they prepare for their more learned Lord.

From hence to NATURES NURSERY they goe;
　　Where seems to grow all that in *Eden* grew;   110
And more (if Art her mingled *Species* show)
　　Then th' Hebrew King, Nature's Historian, knew.

Impatient *Simplers* climbe for Blossomes here;
　　When Dewes (Heav'n's secret milk) in unseen show'rs
First feed the early Childhood of the year;   115
　　And in ripe Summer, stoop for Hearbs and Flow'rs.

In Autumn, Seeds and Berries they provide;
　　Where Nature a remaining force preserves;
In Winter digg for Roots, where she does hide
　　That stock, which if consum'd, the next Spring sterves.   120

From hence (fresh Nature's flourishing Estate!)
　　They to her wither'd Receptacle come;
Where she appears the loathsome Slave of Fate;
　　For here her various Dead possess the Room.

This dismall Gall'ry, lofty, long, and wide;   125
     Was hung with *Skelitons* of ev'ry kinde;
Humane, and all that learned humane pride
     Thinks made t' obey Man's high immortal Minde.

Yet on that Wall hangs he too, who so thought;
     And she dry'd by him, whom that He obey'd;   130
By her an *El'phant* that with Heards had fought,
     Of which the smallest Beast made her afraid.

Next it, a Whale is high in Cables ty'd,
     Whose strength might Herds of Elephants controul;
Then all, (in payres of ev'ry kinde) they spy'd   135
     Which Death's wrack leaves, of Fishes, Beasts, and Fowl.

These *Astragon* (to watch with curious Eye
     The diff'rent Tenements of living breath)
Collects, with what far Travailers supply;
     And this was call'd, The Cabinet of Death.   140

Which some the *Monument of Bodies*, name;
     The Arke, which saves from Graves all dying kindes;
This to a structure led, long known to Fame,
     And call'd, The Monument of vanish'd Mindes.

Where, when they thought they saw in well sought Books,   145
     Th' assembled soules of all that Men held wise,
It bred such awfull rev'rence in their looks,
     As if they saw the bury'd writers rise.

Such reaps of written thoughts (Gold of the Dead,
     Which Time does still disperse, but not devour)   150
Made them presume all was from Deluge free'd,
     Which long-liv'd-Authors writ ere *Noah's* Show'r.

They saw *Egyptian* Roles, which vastly great,
     Did like faln Pillars lie, and did display
The tale of Natures life, from her first heat,   155
     Till by the Flood o'er-cool'd, she felt decay.

And large as these (for Pens were Pencils then)
     Others that *Egypts* chiefest Science show'd;
Whose River forc'd Geometry on Men,
     Which did distinguish what the *Nyle* o're-flow'd.   160

Near them, in Piles, *Chaldean* Cous'ners lie;
     Who the hid bus'ness of the Stars relate;

Who make a Trade of worship'd Prophesie;
  And seem to pick the Cabinet of Fate.

There *Persian Magi* stand; for wisdom prais'd;   165
  Long since wise Statesmen, now *Magicians* thought;
Altars and Arts are soon to fiction rais'd,
  And both would have, that miracles are wrought.

In a dark Text, these States-men left their Mindes;
  For well they knew, that Monarch's Mistery   170
(Like that of Priests) but little rev'rence findes,
  When they the Curtain op'e to ev'ry Eye.

Behinde this Throng, the talking *Greeks* had place;
  Who Nature turn to Art, and Truth disguise,
As skill does native beauty oft deface;   175
  With *Termes* they charm the weak, and pose the wise.

Now they the *Hebrew*, *Greek* and *Roman* spie;
  Who for the Peoples ease, yoak'd them with Law;
Whom else, ungovern'd lusts would drive awry;
  And each his own way frowardly would draw.   180

In little Tomes these grave first Lawyers lie,
  In Volumes their Interpreters below;
Who first made Law an Art, then Misterie;
  So cleerest springs, when troubled, cloudy grow.

But here, the Souls chief Book did all precede;   185
  Our Map tow'rds Heav'n; to common Crowds deny'd;
Who proudly aim to teach, ere they can read;
  And all must stray, where each will be a Guide.

About this sacred little Book did stand
  Unweildly Volumes, and in number great;   190
And long it was since any Readers hand
  Had reach'd them from their unfrequented Seat.

For a deep Dust (which Time does softly shed,
  Where only Time does come) their Covers beare;
On which, grave Spyders, streets of Webbs had spread;   195
  Subtle, and slight, as the grave Writers were.

In these, Heav'ns holy Fire does vainly burn;
  Nor warms, nor lights, but is in Sparkles spent;
Where froward Authors, with disputes, have torn
  The Garment seamless as the Firmament.   200

These are the old *Polemicks*, long since read,
  And shut by *Astragon*; who thought it just,
They, like the Authors (Truth's Tormentors) dead,
  Should lie unvisited, and lost in dust.

Here the *Arabian's* Gospel open lay,   205
  (Men injure Truth, who Fiction nicely hide)
Where they the *Monk's* audacious stealths survey,
  From the World's first, and greater second Guide.

The Curious much perus'd this, then, new Book;
  As if some secret wayes to Heav'n it taught;   210
For straying from the old, men newer look,
  And prise the found, not finding those they sought.

We, in Tradition (Heav'n's dark Mapp) descrie
  Heav'n worse, then ancient Mapps farr *India* show;
Therefore in new, we search where Heav'n does lie;   215
  The Mind's sought Ophir, which we long to know.

Or as a Planter, though good Land he spies,
  Seeks new, and when no more so good he findes,
Doubly esteems the first; so Truth men prise;
  Truth, the discov'ry made by trav'ling Mindes.   220

And this false Book, till truly understood
  By *Astragon*, was openly display'd;
As counterfeit; false Princes, rather shou'd
  Be shewn abroad, then in close Prison lay'd.

Now to the old *Philosophers* they come;   225
  Who follow'd Nature with such just despaire,
As some do Kings farr off; and when at home,
  Like Courtiers, boast, that they deep secrets share.

Near them are grave dull *Moralists*, who give
  Counsell to such, as still in publick dwell;   230
At sea, in Courts, in Camps, and Citties live;
  And scorn experience from th' unpractis'd Cell.

Esop with these stands high, and they below;
  His pleasant wisdome mocks their gravity;
Who Vertue like a tedious Matron show,   235
  He dresses Nature to invite the Eye.

High skill their *Ethicks* seemes, whilst he stoops down
  To make the People wise; their learned pride

Makes all obscure, that Men may prise the Gown;
    With ease he teaches, what with pain they hide.   240

And next (as if their bus'ness rul'd Mankinde)
    Historians stand, bigg as their living looks;
Who thought, swift Time they could in fetters binde;
    Till his Confessions they had ta'ne in Books:

But Time oft scap'd them in the shades of Night;   245
    And was in Princes Closets oft conceal'd,
And hid in Battels smoke; so what they Write
    Of Courts and Camps, is oft by guess reveal'd.

Near these, *Physitians* stood; who but reprieve
    Like life a Judge, whom greater pow'r does awe;   250
And cannot an Almighty pardon give;
    So much yields Subject Art to Nature's Law.

And not weak Art, but Nature we upbraid,
    When our frail essence proudly we take ill;
Think we are robb'd, when first we are decay'd,   255
    And those were murder'd whom her law did kill.

Now they refresh, after this long survey,
    With pleasant *Poets*, who the Soul sublime;
Fame's *Heraulds*, in whose Triumphs they make way;
    And place all those whom Honor helps to climbe.   260

And he who seem'd to lead this ravish'd Race,
    Was Heav'n's lov'd *Laureat*, that in *Jewry* writ;
Whose Harp approach'd Gods Ear, though none his Face
    Durst see, and first made inspiration, wit.

And his Attendants, such blest Poets are,   265
    As make unblemish'd Love, Courts best delight;
And sing the prosp'rous Battels of just warre;
    By these the loving, Love, and valiant, fight.

O hireless Science! and of all alone
    The Liberal! Meanly the rest each State   270
In pension treats, but this depends on none;
    Whose worth they rev'rendly forbear to rate.

SIR JOHN DENHAM

(1615-1642-1669)

Cooper's Hill[1]

SURE there are Poets which did never dream
Upon *Parnassus*, nor did tast the stream
Of *Helicon*, we therefore may suppose
Those made no Poets, but the Poets those.
And as Courts make not Kings, but Kings the Court,   5
So where the Muses & their train resort,
Parnassus stands; if I can be to thee
A Poet, thou *Parnassus* are to me.
Nor wonder, if (advantag'd in my flight,
By taking wing from thy auspicious height)   10
Through untrac't ways, and aery paths I fly,
More boundless in my Fancy than my eie:
My eye, which swift as thought contracts the space
That lies between, and first salutes the place
Crown'd with that sacred pile, so vast, so high,   15
That whether 'tis a part of Earth, or sky,
Uncertain seems, and may be thought a proud
Aspiring mountain, or descending cloud,
Pauls, the late theme of such a Muse whose flight
Has bravely reach't and soar'd above thy height: 20
Now shalt thou stand though sword, or time, or fire,
Or zeal more fierce than they, thy fall conspire,
Secure, whilst thee the best of Poets sings,
Preserv'd from ruine by the best of Kings.
Under his proud survey the City lies,   25
And like a mist beneath a hill doth rise;
Whose state and wealth the business and the crowd,
Seems at this distance but a darker cloud:
And is to him who rightly things esteems,
No other in effect than what it seems: 30
Where, with like hast, though several ways, they run
Some to undo, and some to be undone;
While luxury, and wealth, like war and peace,
Are each the others ruine, and increase;
As Rivers lost in Seas some secret vein   35
Thence reconveighs, there to be lost again.
Oh happiness of sweet retir'd content!

---

[1] Published in 1642. Text of *Poems and Translations*, 1668.

To be at once secure, and innocent.
Windsor the next (where *Mars* with *Venus* dwells.
Beauty with strength) above the Valley swells   40
Into my eye, and doth it self present
With such an easie and unforc't ascent,
That no stupendious precipice denies
Access, no horror turns away our eyes:
But such a Rise, as doth at once invite   45
A pleasure, and a reverence from the sight.
Thy mighty Masters Embleme, in whose face
Sate meekness, heightned with Majestick Grace
Such seems thy gentle height, made only proud
To be the basis of that pompous load,   50
Than which, a nobler weight no Mountain bears,
But *Atlas* only that supports the Sphears.
When Natures hand this ground did thus advance,
'Twas guided by a wiser power than Chance;
Mark't out for such a use, as if 'twere meant   55
T' invite the builder, and his choice prevent.
Nor can we call it choice, when what we chuse,
Folly, or blindness only could refuse.
A Crown of such Majestick towrs doth Grace
The Gods great Mother, when her heavenly race   60
Do homage to her, yet she cannot boast
Amongst that numerous, and Celestial host,
More *Hero's* than can *Windsor*, nor doth Fames
Immortal book record more noble names.
Not to look back so far, to whom this Isle   65
Owes the first Glory of so brave a pile,
Whether to *Cæsar*, *Albanact*, or *Brute*,
The Brittish *Arthur*, or the Danish *Knute*,
(Though this of old no less contest did move,
Then when for *Homers* birth seven Cities strove)   70
(Like him in birth, thou should'st be like in fame,
As thine his fate, if mine had been his Flame)
But whosoere it was, Nature design'd
First a brave place, and then as brave a mind.
Not to recount those several Kings, to whom   75
It gave a Cradle, or to whom a Tombe,
But thee (great *Edward*) and thy greater son,
(The lillies which his Father wore, he won)
And thy *Bellona*, who the Consort came
Not only to thy Bed, but to thy Fame,   80
She to thy Triumph led one Captive King,
And brought that son, which did the second bring.
Then didst thou found that Order (whither love
Or victory thy Royal thoughts did move)
Each was a noble cause, and nothing less,   85

Than the design, has been the great success:
Which forraign Kings, and Emperors esteem
The second honour to their Diadem.
Had thy great Destiny but given thee skill,
To know as well, as power to act her will,   90
That from those Kings, who then thy captives were,
In after-times should spring a Royal pair
Who should possess all that thy mighty power,
Or thy desires more mighty, did devour;
To whom their better Fate reserves what ere   95
The Victor hopes for, or the Vanquisht fear;
That bloud, which thou and thy great Grandsire shed,
And all that since these sister Nations bled,
Had been unspilt, had happy *Edward* known
That all the bloud he spilt, had been his own.   100
When he that Patron chose, in whom are joyn'd
Souldier and Martyr, and his arms confin'd
Within the Azure Circle, he did seem
But to foretell, and prophesie of him,
Who to his Realms that Azure round hath joyn'd,   105
Which Nature for their bound at first design'd.
That bound, which to the Worlds extreamest ends,
Endless it self, its liquid arms extends;
Nor doth he need those Emblemes which we paint,
But is himself the Souldier and the Saint.   110
Here should my wonder dwell, & here my praise,
But my fixt thoughts my wandring eye betrays,
Viewing a neighbouring hill, whose top of late
A Chappel crown'd, till in the Common Fate,
The adjoyning Abby fell: (may no such storm   115
Fall on our times, where ruine must reform.)
Tell me (my Muse) what monstrous dire offence,
What crime could any Christian King incense
To such a rage? was't Luxury, or Lust?
Was he so temperate, so chast, so just?   120
Were these their crimes? they were his own much more:
But wealth is Crime enough to him that's poor,
Who having spent the Treasures of his Crown,
Condemns their Luxury to feed his own.
And yet this Act, to varnish o're the shame   125
Of sacriledge, must bear devotions name.
No Crime so bold, but would be understood
A real, or at least a seeming good.
Who fears not to do ill, yet fears the Name,
And free from Conscience, is a slave to Fame.   130
Thus he the Church at once protects, & spoils:
But Princes swords are sharper than their stiles.
And thus to th' ages past he makes amends,

Their Charity destroys, their Faith defends.
Then did Religion in a lazy Cell,   135
In empty, airy contemplations dwell;
And like the block, unmoved lay: but ours,
As much too active, like the stork devours.
Is there no temperate Region can be known,
Betwixt their Frigid, and our Torrid Zone?   140
Could we not wake from that Lethargick dream,
But to be restless in a worse extream?
And for that Lethargy was there no cure,
But to be cast into a Calenture?
Can knowledge have no bound, but must advance   145
So far, to make us wish for ignorance?
And rather in the dark to grope our way,
Than led by a false guide to erre by day?
Who sees these dismal heaps, but would demand
What barbarous Invader sackt the land?   150
But when he hears, no Goth, no Turk did bring
This desolation, but a Christian King;
When nothing, but the Name of Zeal, appears
'Twixt our best actions and the worst of theirs,
What does he think our Sacriledge would spare,   155
When such th' effects of our devotions are?
Parting from thence 'twixt anger, shame, & fear,
Those for whats past, & this for whats too near:
My eye descending from the Hill, surveys
Where *Thames* amongst the wanton vallies strays.   160
Thames, the most lov'd of all the Oceans sons,
By his old Sire to his embraces runs,
Hasting to pay his tribute to the Sea,
Like mortal life to meet Eternity.
Though with those streams he no resemblance hold,   165
Whose foam is Amber, and their Gravel Gold;
His genuine, and less guilty wealth t' explore,
Search not his bottom, but survey his shore;
Ore which he kindly spreads his spacious wing,
And hatches plenty for th' ensuing Spring.   170
Nor then destroys it with too fond a stay,
Like Mothers which their Infants overlay.
Nor with a sudden and impetuous wave,
Like profuse Kings, resumes the wealth he gave.
No unexpected inundations spoyl   175
The mowers hopes, nor mock the plowmans toyl:
For God-like his unwearied Bounty flows;
First loves to do, then loves the Good he does.
Nor are his Blessings to his banks confin'd,
But free, and common, as the Sea or Wind;   180
When he to boast, or to disperse his stores

Full of the tributes of his grateful shores,
Visits the world, and in his flying towers
Brings home to us, and makes both *Indies* ours;
Finds wealth where 'tis, bestows it where it wants   185
Cities in deserts, woods in Cities plants.
So that to us no thing, no place is strange,
While his fair bosom is the worlds exchange.
O could I flow like thee, and make thy stream
My great example, as it is my theme!   190
Though deep, yet clear, though gentle, yet not dull,
Strong without rage, without ore-flowing full.
Heaven her *Eridanus* no more shall boast,
Whose Fame in thine, like lesser Currents lost,
Thy Nobler streams shall visit *Jove's* aboads,   195
To shine amongst the Stars, and bath the Gods.
Here Nature, whether more intent to please
Us or her self, with strange varieties,
(For things of wonder give no less delight
To the wise Maker's, than beholders sight.   200
Though these delights from several causes move
For so our children, thus our friends we love)
Wisely she knew, the harmony of things,
As well as that of sounds, from discords springs.
Such was the discord, which did first disperse   205
Form, order, beauty through the Universe;
While driness moysture, coldness heat resists,
All that we have, and that we are, subsists.
While the steep horrid roughness of the Wood
Strives with the gentle calmness of the flood.   210
Such huge extreams when Nature doth unite,
Wonder from thence results, from thence delight.
The stream is so transparent, pure, and clear,
That had the self-enamour'd youth gaz'd here,
So fatally deceiv'd he had not been,   215
While he the bottom, not his face had seen.
But his proud head the aery Mountain hides
Among the Clouds; his shoulders, and his sides
A shady mantle cloaths; his curled brows
Frown on the gentle stream, which calmly flows,   220
While winds and storms his lofty forehead beat:
The common fate of all that's high or great.
Low at his foot a spacious plain is plac't,
Between the mountain and the stream embrac't:
Which shade and shelter from the Hill derives,   225
While the kind river wealth and beauty gives;
And in the mixture of all these appears
Variety, which all the rest indears.
This scene had some bold Greek, or Brittish Bard

Beheld of old, what stories had we heard,   230
Of Fairies, Satyrs, and the Nymphs their Dames,
Their feasts, their revels, & their amorous flames:
'Tis still the same, although their aery shape
All but a quick Poetick sight escape.
There *Faunus* and *Sylvanus* keep their Courts,   235
And thither all the horned hoast resorts,
To graze the ranker mead, that noble heard
On whose sublime and shady fronts is rear'd
Natures great Master-piece; to shew how soon
Great things are made, but sooner are undone.   240
Here have I seen the King, when great affairs
Give leave to slacken, and unbend his cares,
Attended to the Chase by all the flower
Of youth, whose hopes a Nobler prey devour:
Pleasure with Praise, & danger, they would buy,   245
And wish a foe that would not only fly.
The stagg now conscious of his fatal Growth,
At once indulgent to his fear and sloth,
To some dark covert his retreat had made,
Where nor mans eye, nor heavens should invade   250
His soft repose; when th' unexpected sound
Of dogs, and men, his wakeful ear doth wound.
Rouz'd with the noise, he scarce believes his ear,
Willing to think th' illusions of his fear
Had given this false Alarm, but straight his view   255
Confirms, that more than all he fears is true.
Betray'd in all his strengths, the wood beset,
All instruments, all Arts of ruine met;
He calls to mind his strength, and then his speed,
His winged heels, and then his armed head;   260
With these t' avoid, with that his Fate to meet:
But fear prevails, and bids him trust his feet.
So fast he flyes, that his reviewing eye
Has lost the chasers, and his ear the cry;
Exulting, till he finds, their Nobler sense   265
Their disproportion'd speed does recompense.
Then curses his conspiring feet, whose scent
Betrays that safety which their swiftness lent.
Then tries his friends, among the baser herd,
Where he so lately was obey'd, and fear'd,   270
His safety seeks: the herd, unkindly wise,
Or chases him from thence, or from him flies.
Like a declining States-man, left forlorn
To his friends pity, and pursuers scorn,
With shame remembers, while himself was one   275
Of the same herd, himself the same had done.
Thence to the coverts, & the conscious Groves,

The scenes of his past triumphs, and his loves;
Sadly surveying where he rang'd alone
Prince of the soyl, and all the herd his own;   280
And like a bold Knight Errant did proclaim
Combat to all, and bore away the Dame;
And taught the woods to eccho to the stream
His dreadful challenge, and his clashing beam.
Yet faintly now declines the fatal strife;   285
So much his love was dearer than his life.
Now every leaf, and every moving breath
Presents a foe, and every foe a death.
Wearied, forsaken, and pursu'd, at last
All safety in despair of safety plac'd,   290
Courage he thence resumes, resolv'd to bear
All their assaults, since 'tis in vain to fear.
And now too late he wishes for the fight
That strength he wasted in Ignoble flight:
But when he sees the eager chase renew'd,   295
Himself by dogs, the dogs by men pursu'd:
He straight revokes his bold resolve, and more
Repents his courage, than his fear before;
Finds that uncertain waies unsafest are,
And Doubt a greater mischief than Despair.   300
Then to the stream, when neither friends, nor force,
Nor speed, nor Art avail, he shapes his course;
Thinks not their rage so desperate t' assay
An Element more merciless than they.
But fearless they pursue, nor can the floud   305
Quench their dire thirst; alas, they thirst for bloud.
So towards a Ship the oarefin'd Gallies ply,
Which wanting Sea to ride, or wind to fly,
Stands but to fall reveng'd on those that dare
Tempt the last fury of extream despair.   310
So fares the Stagg among th' enraged Hounds,
Repels their force, and wounds returns for wounds.
And as a Hero, whom his baser foes
In troops surround, now these assails, now those,
Though prodigal of life, disdains to die   315
By common hands; but if he can descry
Some nobler foes approach, to him he calls,
And begs his Fate, and then contented falls.
So when the King a mortal shaft lets fly
From his unerring hand, then glad to dy,   320
Proud of the wound, to it resigns his bloud,
And stains the Crystal with a Purple floud.
This a more Innocent, and happy chase,
Than when of old, but in the self-same place,
Fair liberty pursu'd, and meant a Prey   325

To lawless power, here turn'd, and stood at bay.
When in that remedy all hope was plac't
Which was, or should have been at least, the last.
Here was that Charter seal'd, wherein the Crown
All marks of Arbitrary power lays down: 330
Tyrant and slave, those names of hate and fear,
The happier stile of King and Subject bear:
Happy, when both to the same Center move,
When Kings give liberty, and Subjects love.
Therefore not long in force this Charter stood; 335
Wanting that seal, it must be seal'd in bloud.
The Subjects arm'd, the more their Princes gave,
Th' advantage only took the more to crave:
Till Kings by giving, give themselves away,
And even that power, that should deny, betray. 340
"Who gives constrain'd, but his own fear reviles
"Not thank't, but scorn'd; nor are they gifts, but spoils.
Thus Kings, by grasping more than they could hold,
First made their Subjects by oppression bold:
And popular sway, by forcing Kings to give 345
More than was fit for Subjects to receive,
Ran to the same extreams; and one excess
Made both, by striving to be greater, less.
When a calm River rais'd with sudden rains,
Or Snows dissolv'd, oreflows th' adjoyning Plains, 350
The Husbandmen with high-rais'd banks secure
Their greedy hopes, and this he can endure.
But if with Bays and Dams they strive to force
His channel to a new, or narrow course;
No longer then within his banks he dwells, 355
First to a Torrent, then a Deluge swells:
Stronger, and fiercer by restraint he roars,
And knows no bound, but makes his power his shores.

Natura Naturata[1]

WHAT gives us that Fantastick Fit,
That all our Judgment and our Wit
To vulgar custom we submit?

Treason, Theft, Murther, all the rest
Of that foul Legion we so detest, 5
Are in their proper names exprest.

---

[1] Published in *Poems and Translations*, 1668. Text of first edition,

Why is it then taught sin or shame,
Those necessary parts to name,
From whence we went, and whence we came?

Nature, what ere she wants, requires;   10
With Love enflaming our desires,
Finds Engines fit to quench those fires:

Death she abhors; yet when men die,
We are present; but no stander by
Looks on when we that loss supply: 15

Forbidden Wares sell twice as dear;
Even Sack prohibited last year,
A most abominable rate did bear.

'Tis plain our eyes and ears are nice,
Only to raise by that device,   20
Of those Commodities the price.

Thus Reason's shadows us betray
By Tropes and Figures led astray,
From Nature, both her Guide and way.

EDMUND WALLER

(1606-1645-1687)

To the King on His Navy[1]

WHERE e're thy Navy spreads her canvas wings,
Homage to thee, and Peace to all she brings.
The *French* and *Spaniard*, when thy Flags appear,
Forget their Hatred, and consent to fear.
So *Jove* from *Ida* did both Hosts survey,   5
And when he pleas'd to Thunder, part the fray.
Ships heretofore in Seas like Fishes sped,
The mighty still upon the smaller fed.
Thou on the deep imposest Nobler Laws,
And by that Justice hath remov'd the Cause   10
Of those rude Tempests, which for Rapine sent,

---

[1] Published in *Poems*, 1645. Text of *Poems*, *&c. Written upon Several Occasions*,
5th ed., 1686.

Too oft alas, involv'd the innocent.
Now shall the Ocean, as thy *Thames*, be free
From both those fates, of Storms, and Piracy:
But we most happy, who can fear no force   15
But winged Troops, or Pegasean Horse:
'Tis not so hard for greedy foes to spoil
Another Nation, as to touch our soil.
Should Natures self invade the World again,
And o're the Center spread the liquid Main;   20
Thy power were safe, and her destructive hand
Would but enlarge the bounds of thy command.
Thy dreadful Fleet would stile thee Lord of all,
And ride in Triumph o're the drowned Ball.
Those Towers of Oak o're fertile plains might go, 25
And visit Mountains where they once did grow.
    The Worlds Restorer never could endure,
That finish'd *Babel* should those men secure,
Whose Pride design'd that Fabrick to have stood
Above the reach of any second Flood: 30
To thee his Chosen more indulgent, he
Dares trust such Power with so much Piety.

The Battle of the Summer-Islands[1]

Canto I

What Fruits they have, and how Heaven smiles
Upon those late discovered Isles.

AID me *Bellona*, while the dreadful Fight
Betwixt a Nation and two Whales I write:
Seas stained with goar, I sing, advent'rous toyl,
And how these Monsters did disarm an Isle.
    Bermudas wall'd with Rocks, who does not know, 5
That happy Island, where huge Lemons grow,
And Orange trees which Golden Fruit do bear,
Th' Hesperian Garden boasts of none so fair?
Where shining Pearl, Coral, and many a pound,
On the rich Shore, of Amber-greece is found: 10
The lofty Cedar, which to Heaven aspires,
The Prince of Trees, is fewel for their Fires:
The smoak by which their loaded spits do turn,
For incense might, on Sacred Altars burn:

---

[1] Published in *Poems*, 1645. Text of *Poems, &c. Written upon Several Occasions*, 5th ed., 1686.

Their private Roofs on od'rous Timber born,   15
Such as might Palaces for Kings adorn.
The sweet *Palmettas* a new *Bacchus* yield,
With Leaves as ample as the broadest shield:
Under the shadow of whose friendly Boughs
They sit carowsing, where their Liquor grows.   20
Figs there unplanted through the Fields do grow,
Such as fierce *Cato* did the *Romans* show,
With the rare Fruit inviting them to spoil
Carthage the Mistriss of so rich a soil.
The naked Rocks are not unfruitful there,   25
But at some constant seasons every year,
Their barren tops with luscious Food abound,
And with the eggs of various Fowls are crown'd:
Tobacco is the worst of things, which they
To *English* Land-lords as their Tribute pay: 30
Such is the Mould, that the Blest Tenant feeds
On precious Fruits, and pays his Rent in Weeds:
With candid Plantines, and the jucy Pine,   ⎫
On choicest Melons and sweet Grapes they dine; ⎬
And with Potatoes fat their wanton Swine.   ⎭   35
Nature these Cates with such a lavish hand
Pours out among them, that our courser Land
Tastes of that bounty, and does Cloth return,
Which not for Warmth, but Ornament is worn:
For the king Spring which but salutes us here,   40
Inhabits there, and courts them all the year:
Ripe Fruits and blossoms on the same Trees live;
At once they promise, what at once they give:
So sweet the Air, so moderate the Clime;
None sickly lives, or dies before his time.   45
Heaven sure has kept this spot of earth uncurst,
To shew how all things were Created first.
The tardy Plants in our cold Orchards plac'd,
Reserve their Fruit for the next ages taste:
There a small grain in some few Months will be   50
A firm, a lofty, and a spacious Tree:
The *Palma Christi*, and the fair *Papah*,
Now but a seed (preventing Natures law)
In half the Circle of the hasty year
Project a shade, and lovely fruit do wear: 55
And as their Trees in our dull Region set
But faintly grow, and no perfection get;
So in this *Northern* Tract our hoarser Throats
Utter unripe and ill-constrained notes:
Where the supporter of the Poets style,   60
Phœbus, on them eternally does smile.
O how I long! my careless Limbs to lay

Under the Plantanes shade, and all the day
With am'rous Airs my fancy entertain,
Invoke the Muses, and improve my vein!   65
No passion there in my free breast should move,
None but the sweet and best of passions, Love:
There while I sing, if gentle Love be by
That tunes my Lute, and winds the Strings so high,
With the sweet sound of *Sacharissa*'s name,   70
I'll make the listning Savages grow tame.
　　But while I do these pleasing dreams indite,
　　I am diverted from the promis'd fight.

Canto II

Of their alarm, and how their Foes
Discovered were, this Canto *shows.*

THOUGH Rocks so high about this Island rise,
That well they may the num'rous Turk despise;
Yet is no humane fate exempt from fear,
Which shakes their hearts, while through the Isle they hear
A lasting noise, as horrid and as loud   5
As Thunder makes, before it breaks the Cloud.
Three days they dread this murmur, e're they know
From what blind cause th' unwonted sound may grow:
At length Two Monsters of unequal size,
Hard by the shoar a Fisher-man espies;   10
Two mighty Whales, which swelling Seas had tost,
And left them prisoners on the rocky Coast;
One as a Mountain vast, and with her came
A Cub not much inferior to his Dame:
Here in a Pool among the Rocks engag'd,   15
They roar'd like Lions, caught in toyls, and rag'd:
The man knew what they were, who heretofore
Had seen the like lie murdered on the shore,
By the wild fury of some Tempest cast
The fate of ships and shipwrackt men to taste.   20
As careless Dames whom Wine and Sleep betray
To frantick dreams their Infants overlay:
So there sometimes the raging Ocean fails,
And her own brood exposes; when the Whales
Against sharp Rocks like reeling vessels quasht,   25
Though huge as Mountains, are in pieces dasht;
Along the shore their dreadful Limbs lie scatter'd,
Like Hills with Earthquakes shaken, torn & shatter'd.
Hearts sure of Brass they had, who tempted first,
Rude Seas that spare not what themselves have nurst.   30
　　The welcome news through all the Nation spread,

To sudden joy and hope converts their dread.
What lately was their publique terror, they
Behold with glad eyes as a certain prey;
Dispose already of th' untaken spoil,   35
And as the purchase of their future toil,
These share the Bones, and they divide the Oyl;
So was the Huntsman by the Bear opprest,
Whose Hide he sold before he caught the Beast.
  They man their Boats, and all their young men arm   40
With whatsoever may the Monsters harm;
Pikes, Halberts, Spits, and Darts that wound so far,
The Tools of Peace, and Instruments of War:
Now was the time for vig'rous Lads to show
What love or honor could invite them to;   45
A goodly Theatre where Rocks are round
With reverend age, and lovely Lasses crown'd:
Such was the Lake which held this dreadful pair
Within the bounds of noble *Warwicks* share:
Warwicks bold Earl, than which no title bears   50
A greater sound among our British Peers;
And worthy he the memory to renew,
The fate and honor to that title due;
Whose brave adventures have transferr'd his name,
And through the new world spread his growing fame.   55
  But how they fought, & what their valour gain'd,
Shall in another Canto be contain'd.

Canto III

*The bloody fight, successless toyl,
And how the Fishes sack'd the Isle.*

The Boat which on the first assault did go
Struck with a harping Iron the younger fo;
Who when he felt his side so rudely goar'd,
Loud as the Sea that nourish't him he roar'd.
As a broad Bream to please some curious tast,   5
While yet alive in boyling water cast,
Vex't with unwonted heat, boyls, flings about
The scorching brass, and hurls the liquor out:
So with the barbed Javeling stung, he raves,
And scourges with his tayl the suffering waves: 10
Like *Spencer's Talus* with his Iron flayl,
He threatens ruin with his pondrous tayl;
Dissolving at one stroke the battered Boat,
And down the men fall drenched in the Moat:
With every fierce encounter they are forc't   15

To quit their Boats, and fare like men unhorst.
  The bigger Whale like some huge Carrack lay,
Which wanteth Sea room, with her foes to play;
Slowly she swims, and when provok'd she wo'd
Advance her tail, her head salutes the mud;   20
The shallow water doth her force infringe,
And renders vain her tails impetuous swinge:
The shining steel her tender sides receive,
And there like Bees they all their weapons leave.
  This sees the Cub, and does himself oppose   25
Betwixt his cumbred mother and her foes:
With desperate courage he receives her wounds,
And men and boats his active tayl confounds.
Their forces joyn'd, the Seas with billows fill,
And make a tempest, though the winds be still.   30
  Now would the men with half their hoped prey
Be well content, and wish this Cub away:
Their wish they have; he to direct his dam
Unto the gap through which they thither came,
Before her swims, and quits the hostile Lake,   35
A pris'ner there, but for his mothers sake.
She by the Rocks compell'd to stay behind,
Is by the vastness of her bulk confin'd.
They shout for joy, and now on her alone
Their fury falls, and all their Darts are thrown.   40
Their Lances spent; one bolder than the rest
With his broad sword provok'd the sluggish beast:
Her oily side devours both blade and heft,
And there his Steel the bold Bermudian left.
Courage the rest from his example take,   45
And now they change the colour of the Lake:
Blood flows in Rivers from her wounded side,
As if they would prevent the tardy tide,
And raise the flood to that propitious height,
As might convey her from this fatal streight.   50
She swims in blood, and blood do's spouting throw
To Heaven, that Heaven mens cruelties might know.
Their fixed Javelins in her side she wears,
And on her back a grove of Pikes appears:
You would have thought, had you the monster seen   55
Thus drest, she had another Island been.
Roaring she tears the air with such a noise,
(As well resembled the conspiring voice
Of routed Armies, when the field is won)
To reach the ears of her escaped son.   60
He (though a league removed from the fo)
Hastes to her aid; the pious Trojan so
Neglecting for *Creusas* life his own,

Repeats the danger of the burning Town.
The men amazed blush to see the seed 65
Of monsters, human piety exceed:
Well proves this kindness what the Grecians sung,
That Loves bright mother from the Ocean sprung.
Their courage droops, and hopeless now they wish
For composition with th' unconquer'd fish: 70
So she their weapons would restore again,
Through Rocks they'd hew her passage to the main.
But how instructed in each others mind,
Or what commerce can men with monsters find?
Not daring to approach their wounded foe, 75
Whom her couragious son protected so;
They charge their Muskets, and with hot desire
Of full revenge, renew the fight with fire:
Standing a looff, with lead they bruise the scales,
And tear the flesh of the incensed Whales. 80
But no success their fierce endeavours found,
Nor this way could they give one fatal wound.
Now to their Fort they are about to send
For the loud Engines which their Isle defend.
But what those pieces fram'd to batter walls 85
Would have effected on those mighty Whales,
Great *Neptune* will not have us know, who sends
A tyde so high, that it relieves his friends.
And thus they parted with exchange of harms;
Much blood the Monsters lost, and they their Arms. 90

To Phillis[1]

PHILLIS, why should we delay
Pleasures shorter than the day?
Could we (which we never can)
Stretch our lives beyond their span;
Beauty like a shadow flies, 5
And our youth before us dies;
Or would youth and beauty stay,
Love hath wings, and will away.
Love hath swifter wings than Time;
Change in love to Heaven does clime. 10
Gods that never change their state,
Vary oft their love and hate.
Phillis, to this truth we owe,

---

[1] Published in *Poems,* 1645. Text of *Poems, &c. Written upon Several Occasions,* 5th ed., 1686.

All the love betwixt us two:
Let not you and I require, 15
What has been our past desire;
On what Shepherds you have smil'd,
Or what Nymphs I have beguil'd;
Leave it to the Planets too,
What we shall hereafter do; 20
For the joys we now may prove,
Take advice of present love.

On a Girdle[1]

THAT which her slender waste confin'd,
Shall now my joyful Temples bind;
No Monarch but would give his Crown,
His Arms might do what this has done.

It was my Heaven's extreamest Sphear, 5
The Pale which held that lovely Dear;
My Joy, my Grief, my Hope, my Love,
Did all within this Circle move.

A narrow compass, and yet there
Dwelt all that's good, and all that's fair: 10
Give me but what this Riban bound,
Take all the rest the Sun goes round.

Song[2]

Go LOVELY Rose,
Tell her that wastes her time and me,
That now she knows,
When I resemble her to thee,
How sweet and fair she seems to be. 5

Tell her that's young,
And shuns to have her Graces spy'd,
That hadst thou sprung

---

[1] Published in *Poems*, 1645. Text of *Poems, &c. Written upon Several Occasions*, 5th ed., 1686.
[2] Published in *Poems*, 1645. Text of *Poems, &c. Written upon Several Occasions*, 5th ed., 1686.

In Desarts, where no men abide,
  Thou must have uncommended dy'd.   10

  Small is the worth
Of Beauty from the light retir'd;
  Bid her come forth,
Suffer her self to be desir'd,
  And not blush so to be admir'd.   15

  Then die, that she,
The common fate of all things rare,
  May read in thee;
How small a part of time they share,
  That are so wondrous sweet and fair.   20

On St. James's Park, as Lately Improved by His Majesty[1]

Of the first Paradice there's nothing found,
Plants set by Heav'n are vanisht, & the ground;
Yet the description lasts; who knows the fate
Of lines that shall this Paradice relate?
  Instead of Rivers rowling by the side   5
Of *Eden*'s Garden, here flows in the Tyde;
The Sea which always serv'd his Empire, now
Pays Tribute to our Prince's pleasure too:
Of famous Cities we the Founders know;
But Rivers old, as Seas, to which they go,   10
Are Nature's bounty; 'tis of more Renown
To make a River than to build a Town.
For future shade young Trees upon the banks
Of the new stream appear in even ranks:
The voice of *Orpheus* or *Amphion*'s hand   15
In better order could not make them stand;
May they increase as fast, and spread their boughs,
As the high Fame of their great Owner grows!
May he live long enough to see them all
Dark shadows cast, and as his Palace tall.   20
Methinks I see the love that shall be made,
The Lovers walking in that amorous shade,
The Gallants dancing by the Rivers side,
They bathe in Summer, and in Winter slide.

---

[1] Published in 1661. Text of *Poems, &c. Written upon Several Occasions*, 5th ed., 1686.

Methinks I hear the Musick in the Boats,   25
And the loud Eccho which returns the Notes,
Whilst over head a flock of new sprung Fowl
Hangs in the Air, and does the Sun controul:
Darkning the Sky they hover o're, and shrowd
The wanton Sailors with a feather'd cloud: 30
Beneath a shole of silver Fishes glides,
And plays about the gilded Barges sides;
The Ladies angling in the Chrystal Lake,
Feast on the waters with the prey they take;
At once victorious with their Lines and Eyes   35
They make the Fishes and the Men their prize;
A thousand *Cupids* on the Billows ride,
And Sea-Nymphs enter with the swelling Tide,
From *Thetis* sent as Spies to make report,
And tell the wonders of her Soveraign's Court,   40
All that can living feed the greedy Eye,
Or dead the Palat, here you may descry,
The choicest things that furnisht *Noah*'s Ark,
Or *Peter*'s sheet, inhabiting this Park:
All with a border of rich Fruit-trees crown'd,   45
Whose loaded branches hide the lofty mound.
Such various ways the spacious Allies lead,
My doubtful Muse knows not what path to tread:
Yonder the harvest of cold months laid up,
Gives a fresh coolness to the Royal Cup,   50
There Ice, like Chrystal, firm, and never lost,
Tempers hot *July* with *Decembers* Frost,
Winters dark Prison, whence he cannot flie,
Though the warm Spring his enemy draws nigh:
Strange! that extremes should thus preserve the snow   55
High on the *Alps*, or in deep Caves below.
  Here a well-polisht Mall gives us the joy
To see our Prince his matchless force imploy;
His manly posture and his graceful meen
Vigor and Youth in all his motion seen,   60
His shape so lovely, and his limbs so strong,
Confirm our hopes we shall obey him long:
No sooner has he toucht the flying Ball,
But 'tis already more than half the Mall;
And such a fury from his arm has got   65
As from a smoaking Culverin 'twere shot.
  Nere this my Muse, what most delights her, sees,
A living Gallery of aged Trees;
Bold Sons of earth that thrust their arms so high,
As if once more they would invade the Sky;   70

In such green Palaces the first Kings reign'd,
Slept in their shades, and Angels entertain'd:
With such old Counsellors they did advise,
And by frequenting sacred Groves grew wise;
Free from th' impediments of light and noise   75
Man thus retir'd his nobler thoughts imploys:
Here *Charles* contrives the ordering of his States,
Here he resolves his neighb'ring Princes fates:
What Nation shall have Peace, where War be made
Determin'd is in this oraculous shade;   80
The World from *India* to the frozen *North*,
Concern'd in what this Solitude brings forth.
His Fancy objects from his view receives,
The prospect thought and contemplation gives:
That seat of Empire here salutes his eye,   85
To which three Kingdoms do themselves apply,
The structure by a Prelate rais'd, *Whitehall*,
Built with the fortune of *Rome*'s Capitol;
Both disproportion'd to the present State
Of their proud Founders, were approv'd by Fate;   90
From hence he does that antique Pile behold,
Where Royal heads receive the sacred gold;
It gives them Crowns, and does their ashes keep;
There made like gods, like mortals there they sleep
Making the circle of their Reign complete,   95
Those Suns of Empire, where they rise they set:
When others fell, this standing did presage
The Crown should triumph over popular rage,
Hard by that House where all our Ills were shap'd,
Th' auspicious Temple stood, and yet escap'd.   100
So Snow on *Ætna* does unmelted lie,
Whence rowling flames and scatter'd cinders flie;
The distant Countrey in the ruine shares,
What falls from Heav'n the burning Mountain spares.
Next, that capacious Hall he sees the room,   105
Where the whole Nation does for Justice come.
Under whose large roof flourishes the Gown,
And Judges grave on high Tribunals frown.
Here like the peoples Pastor he does go,
His flock subjected to his view below;   110
On which reflecting in his mighty mind,
No private passion does Indulgence find;
The pleasures of his Youth suspended are,
And made a Sacrifice to publick care;
Here free from Court compliances he walks,   115
And with himself, his best adviser, talks;

How peaceful Olive may his Temples shade,
For mending Laws, and for restoring Trade;
Or how his Brows may be with Laurel charg'd,
For Nation's conquer'd, and our Bounds inlarg'd: 120
Of ancient Prudence here he ruminates,
Of rising Kingdoms, and of falling States:
What ruling *Arts* gave Great *Augustus* Fame,
And how *Alcides* purchas'd such a name:
His eyes upon his native Palace bent   125
Close by, suggest a greater argument,
His thoughts rise higher when he does reflect
On what the world may from that Star expect
Which at his Birth appear'd to let us see
Day for his sake could with the Night agree;   130
A Prince on whom such different lights did smile,
Born, the divided world to reconcile:
Whatever Heaven or high extracted blood
Could promise or foretell, he will make good;
Reform these Nations, and improve them more,   135
Than this fair Park from what it was before.

Of the Last Verses in the Book[1]

WHEN we for Age could neither read nor write,
The Subject made us able to indite.
The Soul with Nobler Resolutions deckt,
The Body stooping, does Herself erect:
No Mortal Parts are requisite to raise   5
Her, that Unbody'd can her Maker praise.
    The Seas are quiet, when the Winds give o're;
So calm are we, when Passions are no more:
For then we know how vain it was to boast
Of fleeting Things, so certain to be lost.   10
Clouds of Affection from our younger Eyes
Conceal that emptiness, which Age descries.
    The Soul's dark Cottage, batter'd and decay'd,
Let's in new Light thrô chinks that time has made.
Stronger by weakness, wiser Men become   15
As they draw near to their Eternal home:
Leaving the Old, both Worlds at once they view,
That stand upon the Threshold of the New.
                    —*Miratur Limen Olympi.*
                                    Virgil.

---

[1] Published in *Poems, &c. Written upon Several Occasions*, 5th ed., 1686. Text of first edition.

Song[1]

CHLORIS farewell; I now must go:
   For if with thee I longer stay,
Thy Eyes prevail upon me so,
   I shall prove Blind, and lose my Way.

Fame of thy Beauty, and thy Youth,   5
   Among the rest, me hither brought:
Finding this Fame fall short of Truth,
   Made me stay longer than I thought.

For I'm engag'd by Word, and Oath,
   A Servant to another's Will;   10
Yet, for thy Love, I'd forfeit both,
   Cou'd I be sure to keep it still.

But what Assurance can I take?
   When thou, foreknowing this Abuse,
For some more worthy Lover's sake,   15
   May'st leave me with so just Excuse.

For thou may'st say 'twas not thy Fault
   That thou didst thus inconstant prove,
Being by my Example taught
   To break thy Oath, to mend thy Love.   20

No Chloris, no; I will return,
   And raise thy Story to that height,
That Strangers shall at distance burn,
   And she distrust me Reprobate.

Then shall my Love this doubt displace,   25
   And gain such trust, that I may come
And banquet sometimes on thy Face,
   But make my constant Meals at home.

---

[1] Published in *Poems*, 8th ed., 1711. Text of first edition.

ANDREW MARVELL

(1621-1649-1678)

To His Coy Mistress[1]

HAD we but World enough, and Time,
This coyness Lady were no crime.
We would sit down, and think which way
To walk, and pass our long Loves Day.
Thou by the *Indian Ganges* side   5
Should'st Rubies find: I by the Tide
Of *Humber* would complain. I would
Love you ten years before the Flood:
And you should if you please refuse
Till the Conversion of the *Jews*.   10
My vegetable Love should grow
Vaster than Empires, and more slow.
An hundred years should go to praise
Thine Eyes, and on thy Forehead Gaze.
Two hundred to adore each Breast: 15
But thirty thousand to the rest.
An Age at least to every part,
And the last Age should show your Heart.
For Lady you deserve this State;
Nor would I love at lower rate.   20
    But at my back I alwaies hear
Times winged Charriot hurrying near:
And yonder all before us lye
Desarts of vast Eternity.
Thy Beauty shall no more be found;   25
Nor, in thy marble Vault, shall sound
My ecchoing Song: then Worms shall try
That long preserv'd Virginity:
And your quaint Honour turn to dust;
And into ashes all my Lust.   30
The Grave's a fine and private place,
But none I think do there embrace.
    Now therefore, while the youthful hew
Sits on thy skin like morning lew,
And while thy willing Soul transpires   35
At every pore with instant Fires,

---

[1] Written cir. 1646-50. Published in *Miscellaneous Poems*, 1681. Text of first edition. I have adopted Margoliouth's emendation of "glew" to "lew" (*i.e.*, 'warmth') in l. 34.

Now let us sport us while we may;
And now, like am'rous birds of prey,
Rather at once our Time devour,
Than languish in his slow chapt pow'r.   40
Let us roll all our Strength, and all
Our sweetness, up into one Ball:
And tear our Pleasures with rough strife,
Thorough the Iron gates of Life.
Thus, though we cannot make our Sun   45
Stand still, yet we will make him run.

The Garden[1]

How vainly men themselves amaze
To win the Palm, the Oke, or Bayes;
And their uncessant Labours see
Crown'd from some single Herb or Tree,
Whose short and narrow verged Shade   5
Does prudently their Toyles upbraid;
While all Flow'rs and all Trees do close
To weave the Garlands of repose.

Fair quiet, have I found thee here,
And Innocence thy Sister dear!   10
Mistaken long, I sought you then
In busie Companies of Men.
Your sacred Plants, if here below,
Only among the Plants will grow.
Society is all but rude,   15
To this delicious Solitude.

No white nor red was ever seen
So am'rous as this lovely green.
Fond Lovers, cruel as their Flame,
Cut in these Trees their Mistress name.   20
Little, Alas, they know, or heed,
How far these Beauties Hers exceed!
Fair Trees! where s'eer your barkes I **wound**
No Name shall but your own be found.

When we have run our Passions heat,   25
Love hither makes his best retreat.
The *Gods,* that mortal Beauty chase,

---

[1] Written cir. 1650-52. Published in *Miscellaneous Poems,* 1681. Text of first
edition.

Still in a Tree did end their race.
Apollo hunted *Daphne* so,
Only that She might Laurel grow.   30
And *Pan* did after *Syrinx* speed,
Not as a Nymph, but for a Reed.

What wond'rous Life in this I lead!
Ripe Apples drop about my head;
The Luscious Clusters of the Vine   35
Upon my Mouth do crush their Wine;
The Nectaren, and curious Peach,
Into my hands themselves do reach;
Stumbling on Melons, as I pass,
Insnar'd with Flow'rs, I fall on Grass.   40

Mean while the Mind, from pleasure less,
Withdraws into its happiness:
The Mind, that Ocean where each kind
Does streight its own resemblance find;
Yet it creates, transcending these,   45
Far other Worlds, and other Seas;
Annihilating all that's made
To a green Thought in a green Shade.

Here at the Fountains sliding foot,
Or at some Fruit-trees mossy root,   50
Casting the Bodies Vest aside,
My Soul into the boughs does glide:
There like a Bird it sits, and sings,
Then whets, and combs its silver Wings;
And, till prepar'd for longer flight,   55
Waves in its Plumes the various Light.

Such was that happy Garden-state,
While Man there walk'd without a Mate:
After a Place so pure, and sweet,
What other Help could yet be meet!   60
But 'twas beyond a Mortal's share
To wander solitary there:
Two Paradises 'twere in one
To live in Paradise alone.

How well the skilful Gardner drew   65
Of flow'rs and herbes this Dial new;
Where from above the milder Sun
Does through a fragrant Zodiack run;
And, as it works, th' industrious Bee
Computes its time as well as we.   70

How could such sweet and wholsome Hours
Be reckon'd but with herbs and flow'rs!

Bermudas[1]

WHERE the remote *Bermudas* ride
In th' Oceans bosome unespy'd,
From a small Boat, that row'd along,
The listning Winds receiv'd this Song.
   What should we do but sing his Praise   5
That led us through the watry Maze,
Unto an Isle so long unknown,
And yet far kinder than our own?
Where he the huge Sea-Monsters wracks,
That lift the Deep upon their Backs.   10
He lands us on a grassy Stage;
Safe from the Storms, and Prelat's rage.
He gave us this eternal Spring,
Which here enamells every thing;
And sends the Fowl's to us in care,   15
On daily Visits through the Air.
He hangs in shades the Orange bright,
Like golden Lamps in a green Night.
And does in the Pomgranates close,
Jewels more rich than *Ormus* show's.   20
He makes the Figs our mouths to meet;
And throws the Melons at our feet.
But Apples plants of such a price,
No Tree could ever bear them twice.
With Cedars, chosen by his hand,   25
From *Lebanon*, he stores the Land.
And makes the hollow Seas, that roar,
Proclaime the Ambergris on shoar.
He cast (of which we rather boast)
The Gospels Pearl upon our Coast.   30
And in these Rocks for us did frame
A Temple, where to sound his Name.
Oh let our Voice his Praise exalt,
Till it arrive at Heavens Vault:
Which thence (perhaps) rebounding, may   35
Eccho beyond the *Mexique Bay*.
Thus sung they, in the *English* boat,
An holy and a chearful Note,

---

[1] Written cir. 1653. Published in *Miscellaneous Poems*, 1681. Text of first edition.

And all the way, to guide their Chime,
With falling Oars they kept the time.   40

JOHN DRYDEN

(1631-1650-1700)

Upon the Death of the Lord Hastings[1]

MUST Noble *Hastings* Immaturely die,
(The Honour of his ancient Family?)
Beauty and Learning thus together meet,
To bring a *Winding* for a *Wedding-sheet*?
Must *Vertue* prove *Death's* Harbinger? Must She,   5
With him expiring, feel Mortality?
Is *Death* (Sin's wages) Grace's now? shall Art
Make us more Learned, only to depart?
If Merit be Disease, if Vertue Death;
To be Good, Not to be, who'd then bequeath   10
Himself to Discipline? Who'd not esteem
Labour a Crime, Study self-murther deem?
Our *Noble Youth* now have pretence to be
Dunces securely, Ign'rant healthfully.
Rare Linguist! whose Worth speaks it self; whose Praise, 15
Though not his Own, all *Tongues* Besides do raise:
Then Whom Great *Alexander* may seem less,
Who conquer'd Men, but not their Languages.
In his Mouth Nations speak; his Tongue might be
Interpreter to *Greece, France, Italy.*   20
His native Soyl was the four parts o' th' Earth;
All *Europe* was too narrow for his Birth.
A young Apostle; and (with rev'rence may
I speak 'it) inspir'd with gift of Tongues, as They.
Nature gave him, a Childe, what Men in vain   25
Oft strive, by Art though further'd, to obtain.
His body was an Orb, his sublime Soul
Did move on Vertue's and on Learning's pole:
Whose Reg'lar Motions better to our view,
Then *Archimedes* Sphere, the Heavens did shew.   30
Graces and Vertues, Languages and Arts,
Beauty and Learning, fill'd up all the parts.
Heav'ns Gifts, which do, like falling Stars, appear

---

[1] Published in *Lachrymæ Musarum*, 1650. Text of first edition. See Preface.

Scatter'd in Others; all, as in their Sphear,
Were fix'd and conglobate in's Soul, and thence   35
Shone th'row his Body with sweet Influence;
Letting their Glories so on each Limb fall,
The whole Frame render'd was Celestial.
Come, learned *Ptolomy*, and tryal make,
If thou this Hero's Altitude canst take;   40
But that transcends thy skill; thrice happie all,
Could we but prove thus Astronomical.
Liv'd *Tycho* now, struck with this Ray, (which shone
More bright i' th' Morn then others Beam at Noon)
He'd take his *Astrolabe*, and seek out here   45
What new Star 't was did gild our Hemisphere.
Replenish'd then with such rare Gifts as these,
Where was room left for such a Foul Disease?
The Nations sin hath drawn that Veil which shrouds
Our Day-spring in so sad benighting Clouds.   50
Heaven would no longer trust its Pledge; but thus
Recall'd it; rapt its *Ganymede* from us.
Was there no milder way but the Small Pox,
The very filth'ness of *Pandora's* Box?
So many Spots, like *næves*, our *Venus* soil?   55
One Jewel set off with so many a Foil?
Blisters with pride swell'd, which th'row 's flesh did sprout
Like Rose-buds, stuck i' th' Lilly-skin about.
Each little Pimple had a Tear in it,
To wail the fault its rising did commit: 60
Who, Rebel-like, with their own Lord at strife,
Thus made an Insurrection 'gainst his Life.
Or were these Gems sent to adorn his Skin,
The Cab'net of a richer Soul within?
No Comet need foretel his Change drew on,   65
Whose Corps might seem a *Constellation*.
O had he di'd of old, how great a strife
Had been, who from his Death should draw their Life?
Who should by one rich draught become whate'er
Seneca, Cato, Numa, Cæsar, were: 70
Learn'd, Vertuous, Pious, Great, and have by this
An Universal *Metempsuchosis*.
Must all these ag'd Sires in one Funeral
Expire? All die in one so young, so small?
Who, had he liv'd his life out, his great Fame   75
Had swoln 'bove any *Greek* or *Romane* name?
But hasty Winter, with one blast, hath brought
The hopes of Autumn, Summer, Spring, to nought.
Thus fades the Oak i' th' sprig, i' th' blade the Corn;
Thus, without Young, this *Phœnix* dies, new born.   80
Must then old three-legg'd gray-beards, with their Gout,

Catarrhs, Rheums, Aches, live three Ages out?
Times Offal, onely fit for th' Hospital,
Or t' hang an Antiquaries room withal;
Must Drunkards, Lechers, spent with Sinning, live   85
With such helps as Broths, Possits, Physick give?
None live but such as should die? Shall we meet
With none but Ghostly Fathers in the Street?
Grief makes me rail; Sorrow will force its way;
And Show'rs of Tears, Tempestuous Sighs best lay.   90
The Tongue may fail; but over-flowing Eyes
Will weep out lasting streams of *Elegies*.
   But thou, O *Virgin-widow*, left alone,
Now thy Beloved, Heaven-ravisht *Spouse* is gone,
(Whose skilful Sire in vain strove to apply   95
Med'cines, when thy Balm was no remedy)
With greater then *Platonick* love, O wed
His Soul, tho' not his Body, to thy Bed:
Let that make thee a Mother; bring thou forth
Th' *Ideas* of his Vertue, Knowledge, Worth;   100
Transcribe th' Original in new Copies; give
Hastings o' th' better part: so shall he live
In's Nobler Half; and the great Grandsire be
Of an Heroick Divine Progenie:
An Issue which t' Eternity shall last,   105
Yet but th' Irradiations which he cast.
Erect no *Mausolæums*: for his best
Monument is his Spouses Marble brest.

Heroick Stanzas,
Consecrated to the Memory of His Highness, OLIVER, Late Lord Protector of this Commonwealth, &c.[1]

AND now 'tis time; for their officious haste,
   Who would before have born him to the Sky,
Like eager *Romans* e'er all Rites were past,
   Did let too soon the sacred Eagle fly.

Though our best Notes are Treason to his Fame,   5
   Join'd with the loud Applause of publick Voice,

[1] Published in *Three Poems upon the Death of his late Highnesse Oliver Lord Protector of England* . . . . 1659. Text of *A Poem upon the Death of . . . Oliver* . . . . 1659. On the probability that this edition was really printed in 1692, see Dobell, *John Dryden, Bibliographical Memoranda* (London, 1922), pp. 1-4.

Since Heaven, what Praise we offer to his Name,
    Hath render'd too Authentick by its Choice.

Though in his Praise no Arts can liberal be,
    Since they, whose Muses have the highest flown,   10
Add not to his Immortal Memory;
    But do an Act of Friendship to their own.

Yet 'tis our Duty and our Interest too,
    Such Monuments as we can build, to raise;
Lest all the World prevent what we shou'd do,   15
    And claim a Title in him by their Praise.

How shall I then begin, or where conclude,
    To draw a Fame so truly Circular?
For in a Round, what Order can be shew'd,
    Where all the Parts so equal perfect are?   20

His Grandeur he derived from Heav'n alone,
    For he was great, e'er Fortune made him so;
And Wars, like Mists that rise against the Sun,
    Made him but greater seem, not greater grow.

No borrow'd Bays his Temples did adorn,   25
    But to our Crown he did fresh Jewels bring;
Nor was his Vertue poison'd, soon as born,
    With the too early Thoughts of being King.

Fortune (that easie Mistress of the Young,
    But to her ancient Servants coy and hard)   30
Him, at that Age, her Favourites ranked among,
    When she her best-lov'd *Pompey* did discard.

He, private, marked the Faults of others Sway,
    And set as Sea-marks for himself to shun;
Not like rash Monarchs, who their Youth betray   35
    By Acts their Age too late wou'd wish undone.

And yet Dominion was not his Design;
    We owe that Blessing not to him, but Heav'n,
Which to fair Acts unsought Rewards did join,
    Rewards that less to him, than us, were giv'n.   40

Our former Chiefs, like Sticklers of the War,
    First sought t' inflame the Parties, then to poise:
The Quarrel lov'd, but did the Cause abhor,
    And did not strike to hurt, but make a noise.

War, our Consumption, was their gainful Trade;   45
  We inward bled, whilst they prolong'd our Pain;
He fought to end our Fighting, and assay'd
  To stench the Blood by breathing of the Vein.

Swift and resistless through the Land he pass'd,
  Like that bold *Greek*, who did the East subdue;   50
And made to Battels such Heroick Haste,
  As if on Wings of Victory he flew.

He fought, secure of Fortune, as of fame;
  Till by new Maps, the Island might be shown,
Of Conquests, which he strew'd where-e'er he came,   55
  Thick as the *Galaxy* with Stars are sown.

His palms, tho under Weights they did not stand,
  Still thriv'd; no Winter could his Laurels fade:
Heaven in his Portraict shew'd a Work-man's Hand
  And drew it perfect, yet without a Shade.   60

Peace was the Prize of all his Toil and Care,
  Which War had banish'd and did now restore:
Bolognia's walls thus mounted in the Air,
  To seat themselves more surely than before.

Her Safety, rescued *Ireland*, to him owes;   65
  And treacherous Scotland, to no Int'rest true,
Yet bless'd that Fate which did his Arms dispose,
  Her Land to civilize, as to subdue.

Nor was he like those Stars which only shine,
  When to pale Mariners they Storms portend: 70
He had his calmer Influence, and his Mien
  Did Love and Majesty together blend.

'Tis true, his Count'nance did imprint an Awe,
  And naturally all Souls to his did bow;
As Wands of Divination downward draw,   75
  And point to beds where Sov'raign Gold doth grow.

When, past all Off'rings to *Pheretrian Jove*,
  He *Mars* depos'd and Arms to Gowns made yield,
Successful Counsels did him soon approve
  As fit for close Intrigues as open Field.   80

To suppliant *Holland* he vouchsaf'd a Peace,
  Our once bold Rival in the *British* Main,

Now tamely glad her unjust Claim to cease,
  And buy our Friendship with her Idol, Gain.

Fame of th' asserted Sea, through *Europe* blown,   85
  Made *France* and *Spain* ambitious of his Love;
Each knew that Side must conquer, he wou'd own;
  And for him fiercely, as for Empire, strove.

No sooner was the *French*-Man's Cause embrac'd,
  That the light *Monsieur* the grave *Don* out-weigh'd: 90
His Fortune turn'd the Scale where-e'er 'twas cast,
  Tho' *Indian* mines were in the other laid.

When absent, yet we conquer'd in his Right;
  For tho' some meaner Artist's Skill were shown,
In mingling Colours, or in placing Light,   95
  Yet still the fair Designment was his own.

For from all Tempers he cou'd Service draw
  The worth of each, with its Alloy, he knew;
And, as the Confident of Nature, saw
  How she Complections did divide and brew.   100

Or he their single Vertues did survey,
  By Intuition, in his own large Breast,
Where all the rich *Idea's* of them lay,
  That were the Rule and Measure to the rest.

When such Heroick Vertue Heaven sets out,   105
  The Stars, like Commons, sullenly obey;
Because it drains them, when it comes about;
  And therefore is a Tax they seldom pay.

From this high Spring, our Foreign Conquests flow,
  Which yet more glorious Triumphs do portend;   110
Since their Commencement to his Arms they owe,
  If Springs as high as Fountains may ascend.

He made us Free-men of the Continent,
  Whom Nature did like Captives treat before;
To nobler Preys the *English* Lion sent,   115
  And taught him first in *Belgian* Walks to roar.

That old unquestion'd Pirate of the Land,
  Proud *Rome*, with Dread the Fate of *Dunkirk* heard;
And trembling, wish'd behind more *Alps* to stand,
  Although an *Alexander* were her Guard.   120

By his Command we boldly cross'd the Line
    And bravely fought where Southern Stars arise;
We trac'd the far-fetched Gold unto the Mine,
    And that which brib'd our Fathers, made our Prize.

Such was our Prince, yet own'd a Soul above   125
    The highest Acts it could produce to show:
Thus poor Mechanick Arts in Publick move,
    Whilst the deep Secrets beyond Practice go.

Nor dy'd he when his Ebbing Fame went less,
    But when fresh Laurels courted him to live: 130
He seem'd but to prevent some new Success,
    As if above what Triumphs Earth could give.

His latest Victories still thickest came,
    As near the Centre, Motion does increase;
Till he, press'd down by his own weighty Name,   135
    Did, like the Vestal, under Spoils decease.

But first, the Ocean, as a tribute, sent
    That Giant-Prince of all her Watry Herd;
And th' Isle, when her protecting *Genius* went,
    Upon his Obsequies loud Sighs conferr'd.   140

No Civil Broils have since his Death arose,
    But Faction now, by Habit, does obey;
And Wars have that Respect for his Repose,
    As winds for *Halcyons* when they breed at Sea.

His Ashes in a Peaceful Urn shall rest,   145
    His Name a great Example stands to show,
How strangely high Endeavours may be bless'd,
    Where Piety and Valour jointly go.

Astræa Redux

A Poem On the Happy Restoration and Return of His Sacred Majesty Charles the Second[1]

Now with a general Peace the World was blest,
While Ours, a World divided from the rest,
A dreadful Quiet felt, and worser far

[1] Published in 1660. Text of *Annus Mirabilis* . . . . , 1688.

Than Armes, a sullen Interval of War:
Thus when black Clouds draw down the lab'ring Skies,   5
Ere yet abroad the winged Thunder flies,
An horrid Stillness first invades the ear,
And in that silence We the Tempest fear.
Th' Ambitious *Swede* like restless Billows tost,
On this hand gaining what on that he lost,   10
Though in his life he Blood and Ruine breath'd,
To his now guideless Kingdom Peace bequeath'd.
And Heaven that seem'd regardless of our Fate,
For *France* and *Spain* did Miracles create,
Such mortal Quarrels to compose in Peace   15
As Nature bred and Int'rest did encrease.
We sigh'd to hear the fair *Iberian* Bride
Must grow a Lilie to the Lilies side,
While Our cross Stars deny'd us *Charles* his Bed
Whom Our first Flames and Virgin Love did wed.   20
For his long absence Church and State did groan;
Madness the Pulpit, Faction seiz'd the Throne:
Experienc'd Age in deep despair was lost
To see the Rebel thrive, the Loyal crost:
Youth that with Joys had unacquainted been   25
Envy'd Gray hairs that once good Days had seen:
We thought our Sires, not with their own content,
Had ere we came to age our Portion spent.
Nor could our Nobles hope their bold Attempt
Who ruin'd Crowns would Coronets exempt: 30
For when by their designing Leaders taught
To strike at Pow'r which for themselves they sought,
The Vulgar gull'd into Rebellion, arm'd,
Their blood to action by the Prize was warm'd.
The Sacred Purple then and Scarlet Gown,   35
Like sanguine Dye, to Elephants was shewn.
Thus when the bold *Typhoeus* scal'd the Sky,
And forc'd Great *Jove* from his own Heaven to fly,
(What King, what Crown from Treasons reach is free,
If *Jove* and *Heaven* can violated be?)   40
The lesser Gods that shar'd his prosp'rous State
All suffer'd in the Exil'd Thund'rers Fate.
The Rabble now such Freedom did enjoy,
As Winds at Sea, that use it to destroy:
Blind as the *Cyclops*, and as wild as he,   45
They own'd a lawless savage Libertie,
Like that our painted Ancestors so priz'd
Ere Empires Arts their Breasts had Civiliz'd.
How Great were then Our *Charles* his Woes, who thus
Was forc'd to suffer for Himself and us!   50
He toss'd by Fate, and hurried up and down,

Heir to his Fathers Sorrows, with his Crown,
Could taste no sweets of Youths desired Age,
But found his Life too true a Pilgrimage.
Unconquer'd yet in that forlorn Estate   55
His Manly Courage overcame his Fate.
His Wounds he took like *Romans* on his Breast,
Which by his Virtue were with Laurels drest,
As Souls reach Heav'n while yet in Bodies pent,
So did he live above his Banishment.   60
That Sun, which we beheld with couz'ned eyes,
Within the Water, mov'd along the Skies.
How easie 'tis when Destiny proves kind,
With full spread Sails, to run before the Wind.
But those that 'gainst stiff Gales laveering go,   65
Must be at once resolv'd and skilful too.
He would not like soft *Otho* hope prevent,
But stay'd and suffer'd Fortune to repent.
These Virtues *Galba* in a Stranger sought;
And *Piso* to Adopted Empire brought.   70
How shall I then my doubtful Thoughts express,
That must his Suff'rings both regret and bless!
For when his early Valour Heav'n had crost,
And all at *Worc'ster* but the honour lost,
Forc'd into Exile from his rightful Throne,   75
He made all Countries where he came his own.
And viewing Monarchs secret Arts of sway
A Royal Factor for their Kingdoms lay.
Thus banish'd *David* spent abroad his time,
When to be Gods Anointed was his Crime,   80
And when restor'd made his proud Neighbours rue
Those choise Remarks he from his Travels drew:
Nor is he only by Afflictions shewn
To conquer others Realms, but rule his own:
Recov'ring hardly what he lost before,   85
His Right indears it much, his Purchase more.
Inur'd to suffer ere he came to raign,
No rash procedure will his Actions stain.
To bus'ness ripened by digestive thought,
His future rule is into Method brought: 90
As they who first Proportion understand,
With easie Practice reach a Master's hand.
Well might the Ancient Poets then confer
On Night, the honour'd name of *Counseller*,
Since struck with rayes of prosp'rous Fortune blind,   95
We Light alone in dark Afflictions find.
In such adversities to Scepters train'd,
The name of *Great* his famous Grandsire gain'd:
Who yet a King alone in Name and Right,

With hunger, cold and angry *Jove* did fight;   100
Shock'd by a Covenanting Leagues vast Pow'rs,
As holy and as Catholick as ours:
Till Fortunes fruitless spight had made it known,
Her blows not shook but riveted his Throne.
   Some lazy Ages, lost in Sleep and Ease,   105
No action leave to busie Chronicles;
Such whose supine felicity but makes
In story *Casmes*, in *Epoche's* mistakes;
O're whom *Time* gently shakes his wings of Down,
Till with his silent Sickle they are mown: 110
Such is not *Charles* his too too active age,
Which govern'd by the wild distemper'd rage
Of some black Star infecting all the Skies,
Made him at his own cost like *Adam* wise.
Tremble, ye Nations, who secure before,   115
Laught at those Arms that 'gainst our selves we bore;
Rouz'd by the lash of his own stubborn Tail,
Our Lion now will foreign Foes assail.
With *Alga* who the sacred Altar strows?
To all the Sea-Gods *Charles* an Offering owes: 120
A Bull to thee, *Portunus*, shall be slain,
A Lamb to you the Tempests of the Main:
For those loud Storms that did against him rore,
Have cast his shipwrack'd Vessel on the Shore.
Yet as wise Artists mix their Colours so,   125
That by degrees they from each other go,
Black steals unheeded from the neighb'ring white
Without offending the well couz'ned sight:
So on us stole our blessed change; while we
Th' effect did feel, but scarce the manner see.   130
Frosts that constrain the ground, and birth deny
To Flow'rs, that in its womb expecting lie,
Do seldom their usurping Pow'r withdraw,
But raging Floods persue their hasty Thaw:
Our Thaw was mild, the Cold not chas'd away,   135
But lost in kindly heat of lengthned day.
Heav'n would no bargain for its Blessings drive,
But what we could not pay for, freely give.
The Prince of Peace would, like himself, confer
A Gift unhop'd without the price of war.   140
Yet as he knew his Blessings worth, took care
That we should know it by repeated Pray'r;
Which storm'd the Skies and ravish'd *Charles* from thence,
As Heav'n it self is took by violence.
Booth's forward Valour only serv'd to shew,   145
He durst that duty pay we all did owe:
Th' Attempt was fair; but Heav'ns prefixed hour

Not come; so like the watchful Travellor,
That by the Moons mistaken light did rise,
Lay down again, and clos'd his weary Eyes.   150
'Twas *MONK* whom Providence design'd to loose
Those real bonds false Freedom did impose.
The blessed Saints that watch'd this turning Scene,
Did from their Stars with joyful wonder lean,
To see small Clues draw vastest weights along,   155
Not in their bulk but in their order strong.
Thus Pencils can by one slight touch restore,
Smiles to that changed face that wept before.
With ease such fond *Chymæra's* we persue,
As Fancy frames for Fancy to subdue;   160
But when our selves to action we betake,
It shuns the Mint like Gold that Chymists make:
How hard was then his Task, at once to be,
What in the Body natural we see;
Mans Architect distinctly did ordain   165
The charge of Muscles, Nerves, and of the Brain,
Through viewless Conduits Spirits to dispense
The Springs of Motion from the Seat of Sense.
'Twas not the hasty product of a day,
But the well ripened Fruit of wise delay.   170
He like a patient Angler, er'e he stroak,
Would let them play a while upon the hook.
Our healthful food the Stomach labours thus,
At first embracing what it strait doth crush.
Wise Leeches will not vain Receipts obtrude,   175
While growing Pains pronounce the Humors crude;
Deaf to complaints they wait upon the Ill,
Till some safe *Crisis* authorize their Skill.
Nor could his Acts too close a Vizard wear,
To scape their Eyes whom Guilt had taught to fear,   180
And guard with caution that polluted nest,
Whence Legion twice before was dispossest.
Once Sacred house, which when they entr'd in,
They thought the place could sanctifie a sin;
Like those that vainly hop'd kind Heav'n would wink,   185
While to excess on Martyrs Tombs they drink.
And as devouter *Turks* first warn their Souls
To part, before they taste forbidden Bowls,
So these when their black Crimes they went about,
First timely charm'd their useless Conscience out.   190
Religions Name against it self was made;
The Shadow serv'd the Substance to invade:
Like Zealous Missions, they did Care pretend
Of Souls in shew, but made the Gold their end.
Th' incensed Pow'rs beheld with scorn from high   195

An Heaven so far distant from the Sky,
Which durst, with horses hoofs that beat the Ground
And Martial Brass, bely the Thunders Sound.
'Twas hence at length just Vengeance thought it fit
To speed their Ruin by their impious wit.   200
Thus *Sforza*, curs'd with a too fertile brain,
Lost by his Wiles the Pow'r his Wit did gain.
Henceforth their Fogue must spend at lesser rate,
Than in its Flames to wrap a Nations Fate.
Suffer'd to live, they are like *Helots* set,   205
A virtuous Shame within us to beget.
For by example most we sinn'd before,
And glass-like clearness mixt with frailty bore.
But since reform'd by what we did amiss,
We by our suff'rings learn to prize our bliss.   210
Like early Lovers whose unpractis'd hearts
Were long the May-game of malicious arts,
When once they find their Jealousies were vain,
With double heat renew their Fires again.
'Twas this produc'd the Joy, that hurried o're   215
Such swarms of *English* to the Neighb'ring shore,
To fetch that Prize, by which *Batavia* made
So rich amends for our impoverish'd Trade.
Oh had you seen from *Schevelines* barren Shore,
(Crowded with troops, and barren now no more,)   220
Afflicted *Holland* to his Farewel bring
True Sorrow, *Holland* to regret a King;
While waiting him his Royal Fleet did ride,
And willing Winds to their lowr'd Sails denied.
The wavering Streamers, Flags, and Standart out,   225
The merry Seamens rude but chearful Shout;
And last the Cannons voice that shook the Skies, ⎤
And, as it fares in sudden Extasies,   ⎬
At once bereft us both of Ears and Eyes.   ⎦
The *Naseby*, now no longer *Englands* shame,   230
But better to be lost in *Charles* his name,
(Like some unequal Bride in nobler sheets)
Receives her Lord: The joyful *London* meets
The Princely *York*, himself alone a freight;
The *Swift-sure* groans beneath Great *Glouc'sters* weight.   235
Secure as when the *Halcyon* breeds, with these,
He that was born to drown might cross the Seas.
Heav'n could not own a Providence, and take
The Wealth three Nations ventur'd at a stake.
The same indulgence *Charles* his Voyage bless'd,   240
Which in his right had Miracles confess'd.
The Winds that never Moderation knew,

Afraid to blow too much, too faintly blew;
Or out of breath with joy could not enlarge
Their straightned Lungs, or conscious of their Charge. 245
The British *Amphitryte* smooth and clear,
In richer Azure never did appear;
Proud her returning Prince to entertain
With the submitted Fasces of the Main.
    And welcom now (*Great Monarch*,) to your own; 250
Behold th' approaching Cliffes of *Albion:*
It is no longer Motion cheats your view,
As you meet it, the Land approacheth you.
The Land returns, and in the white it wears
The marks of Penitence and Sorrow bears. 255
But you, whose Goodness your Descent doth shew,
Your Heav'nly Parentage and Earthly too;
By that same Mildness, which your Fathers Crown
Before did ravish, shall secure your own.
Not ty'd to rules of Policy, you find 260
Revenge less sweet than a forgiving mind.
Thus when th' Almighty would to *Moses* give
A sight of all he could behold and live;
A Voice before his Entry did proclaim
Long-suffering, Goodness, Mercy in his Name. 265
Your Pow'r to Justice doth submit your Cause,
Your Goodness only is above the Laws;
Whose rigid Letter while pronounc'd by you
Is softer made. So winds that tempests brew
When through Arabian Groves they take their flight, 270
Made wanton with rich Odours, lose their spight.
And as those Lees, that trouble it, refine
The agitated Soul of Generous Wine,
So tears of Joy for your returning spilt,
Work out and expiate our former Guilt. 275
Methinks I see those Crowds on *Dover's* Strand,
Who in their haste to welcom you to Land
Choak'd up the Beach with their still growing store,
And made a wilder Torrent on the Shore.
While spurr'd with eager thoughts of past Delight, 280
Those who had seen you court a second sight;
Preventing still your Steps, and making hast
To meet you often wheresoe're you past.
How shall I speak of that triumphant Day
When you renew'd the expiring Pomp of *May!* 285
(A Month that owns an Interest in your Name:
You and the Flow'rs are its peculiar Claim.)
That Star that at your Birth shone out so bright,

It stain'd the duller Suns Meridian light,
Did once again its potent Fires renew,   290
Guiding our Eyes to find and worship you.
   And now times whiter Series is begun,
Which in soft Centuries shall smoothly run;
Those Clouds that overcast your Morn shall fly,
Dispell'd to farthest corners of the Sky.   295
Our Nation, with united Int'rest blest,
Not now content to poize, shall sway, the rest.
Abroad your Empire shall no Limits know,
But like the Sea in boundless Circles flow.
Your much lov'd Fleet shall with a wide Command   300
Besiege the petty Monarchs of the Land:
And as Old Time his Off-spring swallow'd down,
Our Ocean in its depths all Seas shall drown.
Their wealthy Trade from Pyrate's Rapine free,
Our Merchants shall no more Advent'rers be: 305
Nor in the farthest East those Dangers fear
Which humble *Holland* must dissemble here.
Spain to your Gift alone her *Indies* owes,
For what the Pow'rful takes not he bestows.
And *France* that did an Exiles Presence fear   310
May justly apprehend you still too near.
At home the hateful names of Parties cease
And factious Souls are weary'd into peace.
The discontented now are only they
Whose Crimes before did your Just Cause betray: 315
Of those your Edicts some reclaim from sins,
But most your Life and Blest Example wins.
Oh happy Prince, whom Heav'n hath taught the way
By paying Vows, to have more Vows to pay!
Oh Happy Age! Oh times like those alone,   320
By Fate reserv'd for Great *Augustus* Throne!
When the joint growth of Arms and Arts foreshew
The World a Monarch, and that Monarch *You*.

To My Honour'd Friend Dr. Charleton on His Learned and Useful Works; and More Particularly This of Stone-heng, by Him Restored to the True Founders[1]

THE longest Tyranny that ever sway'd
Was that wherein our Ancestors betray'd

---
[1] Published in Walter Charleton's *Chorea Gigantum*, 1663. Text of first edition.

Their free-born *Reason* to the *Stagirite*,
And made his Torch their universal Light.
So *Truth*, while onely one suppli'd the State, 5
Grew scarce, and dear, and yet sophisticate.
Until 'twas bought, like Emp'rique Wares, or Charms,
Hard words seal'd up with *Aristotle*'s Armes.
Columbus was the first that shook his Throne;
And found a *Temp'rate* in a *Torrid* Zone: 10
The fevrish aire fann'd by a cooling breez,
The fruitful Vales set round with shady Trees;
And guiltless *Men*, who danc'd away their time,
Fresh as their *Groves* and *Happy* as their *Clime.*
Had we still paid that homage to a *Name*, 15
Which onely *God* and *Nature* justly claim;
The *Western* Seas had been our utmost bound,
Where *Poets* still might dream the *Sun* was drown'd:
And all the *Starrs*, that shine in *Southern* Skies,
Had been admir'd by none but *Salvage* Eyes. 20
   Among th' *Assertors* of free Reason's claim,
Th' *English* are not the least in Worth, or Fame.
The World to *Bacon* does not onely owe
Its *present* Knowledge, but its *future* too.
Gilbert shall live, till *Lode-stones* cease to draw, 25
Or *British* Fleets the boundless Ocean awe.
And noble *Boyle*, not less in *Nature* seen,
Than his great *Brother* read in *States* and *Men.*
The *Circling* streams, once thought but pools, of blood
(Whether Life's fewel or the Bodie's food) 30
From dark Oblivion *Harvey*'s name shall save;
While *Ent* keeps all the honour that he gave.
Nor are *You*, Learned Friend, the least renown'd;
Whose Fame, not circumscrib'd with *English* ground,
Flies like the nimble journeys of the Light; 35
And is, like that, unspent too in its flight.
Whatever *Truths* have been, by *Art*, or *Chance*,
Redeem'd from *Error*, or from *Ignorance*,
Thin in their *Authors*, (like rich veins of Ore)
Your Works unite, and still discover more. 40
Such is the healing virtue of Your Pen,
To perfect Cures on *Books*, as well as *Men.*
Nor is This Work the least: You well may give
To *Men* new vigour, who makes *Stones* to live.
Through You, the *DANES* (their short Dominion lost) 45
A longer Conquest than the *Saxons* boast.
Stone-heng, once thought a *Temple*, You have found
A *Throne*, where Kings, our Earthly Gods, were Crown'd.

Where by their wondring Subjects They were seen,
Joy'd with their Stature and their Princely meen.   50
Our *Soveraign* here above the rest might stand;
And here be chose again to rule the Land.
    These Ruines sheltered once *His* Sacred Head,
Then when from *Wor'sters* fatal Field *He* fled;
Watch'd by the Genius of this Royal place,   55
And mighty Visions of the Danish Race.
His *Refuge* then was for a *Temple* shown:
But, *He* Restor'd, 'tis now become a *Throne*.

Song[1]

You charm'd me not with that fair face
    Though it was all Divine:
To be another's is the Grace,
    That makes me wish you mine.
The God's and Fortune take their part   5
    Who like young Monarchs fight;
And boldly dare invade that Heart
    Which is another's right.
First mad with hope we undertake
    To pull up every Bar;   10
But once possess'd, we faintly make
    A dull defensive War.
Now every friend is turn'd a foe
    In hope to get our store:
And passion makes us Cowards grow,   15
    Which made us brave before.

Song[2]

Calm was the Even, and clear was the Sky,
    And the new budding Flowers did spring,
When all alone went *Amyntas* and I
    To hear the sweet Nightingal sing;
I sate, and he laid him down by me;   5
    But scarcely his breath he could draw;
For when with a fear, he began to draw near,
    He was dash'd with A ha ha ha ha!

---

[1] Published in *An Evening's Love: or, The Mock-Astrologer*, 1668, Act II, Scene i.
Text of *Plays*, 1701.
    [2] Published in *An Evening's Love: or, The Mock-Astrologer*, 1668, Act IV, Scene i.
Text of *Plays*, 1701.

He blush'd to himself, and lay still for a while,
   And his modesty curb'd his desire;   10
But streight I convinc'd all his fear with a smile,
   Which added new Flames to his Fire.
O *Sylvia*, said he, you are cruel,
   To keep your poor Lover in awe;
Then once more he prest with his hand to my breast,   15
   But was dash'd with A ha ha ha ha!

I knew 'twas his passion that caus'd all his fear;
   And therefore I pity'd his Case:
I whisper'd him softly, there's no Body near,
   And laid my Cheek close to his Face: 20
But as he grew bolder and bolder,
   A Shepherd came by us and saw;
And just as our bliss we began with a Kiss,
   He laugh'd out with A ha ha ha ha!

The Zambra Dance[1]

   Beneath a Myrtle Shade,
Which Love for none but happy Lovers made,
I slept, and straight my Love before me brought
Phillis, the Object of my waking Thought:
Undress'd she came my Flames to meet,   5
While Love strow'd Flow'rs beneath her Feet;
Flow'rs, which so press'd by her, became more sweet.

   From the bright Vision's Head
A careless Veil of Lawn was loosely spread:
From her white Temples fell her shaded Hair,   10
Like cloudy Sun-shine, not too Brown nor Fair.
Her Hands her Lips did Love inspire;
Her every Grace my Heart did fire:
But most her Eyes, which languish'd with desire.

   Ah, Charming Fair, said I,   15
How long can you my Bliss and yours deny?
By Nature and by Love this lovely Shade
Was for Revenge of suffering Lovers made.
Silence and Shades with Love agree:
Both Shelter you, and Favour me;   20
You cannot Blush, because I cannot see.

---

[1] Published in *The Conquest of Granada*, Part I, 1672, Act III, Scene i. Text of *Plays*, 1701.

No, let me Die, she said,
Rather than lose the spotless name of Maid:
Faintly methought she spoke, for all the while
She bid me not believe her, with a Smile.   25
Then Die, said I, she still deny'd:
And, is it thus, thus, thus she cry'd,
You use a harmless Maid! and so she Dy'd.

I wak'd, and straight I knew
I lov'd so well, it made my Dream prove true: 30
Fancy, the kinder Mistriss of the two,
Fancy had done what *Phillis* wou'd not do.
Ah, Cruel Nymph! cease your Disdain;
While I can Dream, you scorn in vain:
Asleep or waking, you must ease my pain.   35

Epilogue[1]

THEY, who have best succeeded on the Stage,
Have still conform'd their Genius to their Age.
Thus *Johnson* did Mechanique humour show,
When Men were dull, and Conversation low.
Then, Comedy was Faultless, but 'twas course: 5
Cobb's Tankard was a Jest, and *Otter's* Horse.
And as their Comedy, their Love was mean;
Except, by chance, in some one Labour'd Scene,
Which must attone for an ill-written Play.
They rose; but at their height could seldom stay.   10
Fame then was cheap, and the first comer sped;
And they have kept it since, by being dead.
But were they now to write, when Critiques weigh
Each Line, and ev'ry Word, throughout a Play,
None of 'em, no not *Johnson* in his height,   15
Could pass, without allowing grains for weight.
Think it not Envy that these Truths are told;
Our Poet's not Malicious, though he's Bold.
'Tis not to brand 'em that their faults are shown,
But, by their Errors, to excuse his own.   20
If Love and Honour now are higher rais'd,
'Tis not the Poet, but the Age is prais'd.
Wit's new arriv'd to a more high degree;
Our Native Language more refin'd and free.
Our Ladies and our Men now speak more wit   25
In Conversation, than those Poets writ.

---

[1] Published in *The Conquest of Granada*, Part II, 1672. Text of *Plays*, 1701.

Then, one of these is, consequently, true;
That what this Poet writes comes short of you,
And imitates you ill, (which most he fears)
Or else his Writing is not worse than theirs.   30
Yet, though you judge, (as sure the Criticks will)
That some before him writ with greater skill:
In this one Praise he has their Fame surpast,
To please an Age more Gallant than the last.

Song[1]

WHY should a foolish Marriage Vow,
   Which long ago was made,
Oblige us to each other now
   When Passion is decay'd?
We lov'd, and we lov'd, as long as we cou'd,   5
   Till our Love was lov'd out in us both:
But our Marriage is dead, when the Pleasure is fled:
   'Twas Pleasure first made it an Oath.

If I have Pleasures for a Friend,
   And farther Love in store,   10
What Wrong has he whose Joys did end,
   And who cou'd give no more?
'Tis a Madness that he should be jealous of me,
   Or that I shou'd bar him of another:
For all we can gain, is to give our selves Pain,   15
   When neither can hinder the other.

Prologue[2]

OUR Author by experience finds it true,
'Tis much more hard to please himself, than you:
And out of no feign'd Modesty, this day,
Damns his Laborious Trifle of a Play:
Not that its worse than what before he writ,   5
But he has now another taste of Wit;
And to confess a Truth, (though out of time)
Grows weary of his long-lov'd Mistriss, Rhyme.
Passion's too fierce to be in Fetters bound,
And Nature flies him like Enchanted Ground.   10

---

[1] Published in *Marriage A-la Mode*, 1673, Act I, Scene i. Text of *Plays*, 1701.
[2] Published in *Aureng-Zebe: or, The great Mogul*, 1676. Text of *Plays*, 1701.

What Verse can do, he has perform'd in this,
Which he presumes the most correct of his.
But spite of all his Pride, a secret Shame
Invades his Breast at *Shakespear*'s sacred Name:
Aw'd when he hears his God-like *Romans* Rage,   15
He, in a just despair, would quit the Stage.
And to an Age less polish'd, more unskill'd,
Does, with disdain, the foremost Honours yield,
As with the greater dead he dares not strive,
He would not match his Verse with those who live: 20
Let him retire, betwixt two Ages cast,
The first of this, and hindmost of the Last.
A losing Gamester, let him sneak away;
He bears no ready Money from the Play.
The Fate which governs Poets thought it fit,   25
He should not raise his Fortunes by his Wit.
The Clergy thrive, and the litigious Bar;
Dull Heroes fatten with the spoils of War;
All Southern Vices, Heav'n be prais'd are here;
But Wit's a Luxury you think too dear.   30
When you to cultivate the Plant are loth,
'Tis a shrewd sign 'twas never of your growth:
And Wit in Northern Climates will not blow,
Except, like *Orange-Trees* 'tis Hous'd from Snow.
There needs no care to put a Play-House down,   35
'Tis the most desart Place of all the Town.
Wit and our Neighbours, to speak proudly, are
Like Monarchs, ruin'd with expensive War.
While, like wise *English*, unconcern'd, you sit,
And see us play the Tragedy of Wit.   40

A Song from the Italian[1]

By A dismal Cypress lying,
Damon cry'd, all pale and dying,
Kind is Death that ends my pain,
But cruel She I lov'd in vain.
The Mossy Fountains   5
Murmure my trouble,
And hollow Mountains
My groans redouble:
Every Nymph mourns me,
Thus while I languish;   10

---

[1] Published in *Limberham: or, The Kind Keeper*, 1678, Act III, Scene i. Text of
Plays, 1701.

She only scorns me,
Who caus'd my anguish.
No Love returning me, but all hope denying;
By a dismal Cypress lying,
Like a Swan, so sung he dying: 15
Kind is Death that ends my pain,
But cruel She I lov'd in vain.

Prologue[1]

SEE my lov'd *Britons*, see your *Shakespear* rise,
An awful Ghost confess'd to human Eyes!
Unman'd, methinks, distinguish'd I had been,
From other Shades, by this eternal Green,
About whose Wreaths the vulgar Poets strive,   5
And with a touch their wither'd Bays revive.
Untaught, unpractis'd in a barbarous Age,
I found not but created first the Stage.
And, if I drain'd no *Greek* or *Latin* store,
'Twas, that my own abundance gave me more.   10
On Foreign Trade I needed not rely,
Like fruitful *Britan*, rich without supply.
In this my rough-drawn Play, you shall behold
Some Master-strokes, so manly and so bold,
That he, who meant to alter, found 'em such,   15
He shook; and thought it Sacrilege to touch.
Now, where are the Successors to my Name?
What bring they, to fill out a Poet's Fame?
Weak, short-liv'd Issues of a feeble Age;
Scarce living to be Christen'd on the Stage!   20
For Humour, Farce; for Love, they Rhyme dispence.
That tolls the Knell for their departed sense.
Dulness might thrive in any Trade but this:
'Twou'd recommend to some fat Benefice.
Dulness, that in a Play-house meets disgrace   25
Might meet with Reverence in its proper place.
The fulsome clench that nauseates the Town ⎫
Wou'd from a Judge or Alderman go down! ⎬
Such virtue is there in a Robe and Gown! ⎭
And that insipid stuff which here you hate, ⎫   30
Might somewhere else be call'd a grave debate: ⎬
Dulness is decent in the Church and State. ⎭
But I forget that still 'tis understood,
Bad Plays are best decry'd by showing good:

---

[1] Published in *Troilus and Cressida*, 1679. Text of *Plays*, 1701.

Sit silent then, that my pleas'd Soul may see   35
A judging Audience once, and worthy me:
My faithful Scene from true Records shall tell
How *Trojan* Valour did the *Greek* excell;
Your great Forefathers shall their Fame regain,
And *Homer*'s angry Ghost repine in vain.   40

Song[1]

Can Life be a blessing,
Or worth the possessing,
Can life be a blessing if love were away?
Ah no! though our love all Night keep us waking,
And though he torment us with Cares all the Day,   5
Yet he sweetens, he sweetens our pains in the taking.
There's an hour at the last, there's an hour to repay.

In every possessing,
The ravishing blessing,
In every possessing the fruit of our pain,   10
Poor Lovers forget long Ages of anguish,
Whate'er they have suffer'd and done to obtain;
'Tis a pleasure, a pleasure to sigh and to languish,
When we hope, when we hope to be happy again.

Prologue[2]

If yet there be a few that take delight
In that which reasonable Men should write,
To them Alone we Dedicate this Night.
The Rest may satisfie their curious Itch
With City Gazets, or some Factious Speech,   5
Or what-ere Libel, for the Publick Good,
Stirs up the Shrove-tide Crew to Fire and Blood!
Remove your Benches, you apostate Pit,
And take Above, twelve penny-worth of Wit;
Go back to your dear Dancing on the Rope,   10
Or see what's worse, the Devil and the Pope!
The Plays that take on our Corrupted Stage,
Methinks, resemble the distracted Age;
Noise, Madness, all unreasonable Things,

---

[1] Published in *Troilus and Cressida*, 1679, Act III, Scene ii. Text of *Plays*, 1701.
[2] Published in Nahum Tate's *The Loyal General*, 1680. Text of first edition.

That strike at Sense, as Rebels do at Kings! 15
The stile of Forty One our Poets write,
And you are grown to judge like Forty Eight.
Such Censures our mistaking Audience make,
That 'tis almost grown Scandalous to Take!
They talk of Feavours that infect the Brains, 20
But Non-sence is the new Disease that reigns.
Weak Stomachs, with a long Disease opprest,
Cannot the Cordials of strong Wit digest;
Therefore thin Nourishment of Farce ye choose,
Decoctions of a Barly-water Muse: 25
A Meal of Tragedy wou'd make ye Sick,
Unless it were a very tender Chick.
Some Scenes in Sippets wou'd be worth our time,
Those wou'd go down; some Love that's poach'd in Rime;
If these shou'd fail— 30
We must lie down, and, after all our cost,
Keep Holy-day, like Water-men in Frost;
Whilst you turn Players on the Worlds great Stage,
And Act your selves the Farce of your own Age.

Absalom and Achitophel. A Poem[1]

In pious times, e'r Priest-craft did begin,
Before *Polygamy* was made a Sin;
When Man on many multipli'd his kind,
E'r one to one was cursedly confin'd,
When Nature prompted and no Law deni'd 5
Promiscuous Use of Concubine and Bride;
Then *Israel's* Monarch, after Heavens own heart,
His vigorous warmth did, variously, impart
To Wives and Slaves: And, wide as his Command,
Scatter'd his Maker's Image through the Land. 10
Michal,[2] of Royal Blood, the Crown did wear,
A soil ungrateful to the Tiller's care:
Not so the rest; for several Mothers bore
To God-like *David*[3] several sons before.
But since like Slaves his Bed they did ascend, 15
No True Succession could their Seed attend.
Of all this Numerous Progeny was none
So Beautiful so Brave as *Absalon*:[4]
Whether, inspird by some diviner Lust,

---

[1] Published in November, 1681. Text of second edition, December, 1681. See Preface.
[2] Queen Katharine.
[3] Charles II.
[4] The Duke of Monmouth.

His father got him with a greater Gust,   20
Or that his Conscious Destiny made way
By manly Beauty to Imperial Sway.
Early in Foreign Fields he won Renown
With Kings and States allied to *Israel's* Crown:
In Peace the thoughts of War he coud remove   25
And seem'd as he were onely born for Love.
What e'r he did was done with so much ease,
In him alone, 'twas Natural to please;
His motions all accompanied with grace;
And *Paradise* was open'd in his face.   30
With secret Joy, indulgent *David* view'd
His Youthful Image in his Son renew'd;
To all his wishes Nothing he deni'd
And made the Charming *Annabel* his Bride.
What faults he had (for who from faults is free?)   35
His father coud not or he woud not see.
Some warm excesses, which the Law forbore,
Were constru'd Youth that purg'd by boiling o'r:
And *Amnon's* Murther, by a specious Name,
Was call'd a Just Revenge for injur'd Fame.   40
Thus Prais'd and Lov'd, the Noble Youth remain'd,
While *David*, undisturb'd, in *Sion* reign'd.
But Life can never be sincerely blest:
Heav'n punishes the bad, and proves the best.
The *Jews*, a Headstrong, Moody, Murm'ring race   45
As ever tri'd th' extent and stretch of grace;
God's pamper'd People, whom, debauch'd with ease,
No King could govern nor no God could please;
(Gods they had tri'd of every shape and size
That God-smiths could produce or Priests devise:)   50
These *Adam*-wits, too fortunately free,
Began to dream they wanted liberty;
And when no rule, no president was found
Of men, by Laws less circumscrib'd and bound;
They led their wild desires to Woods and Caves;   55
And thought that all but Savages were Slaves.
They who, when *Saul* was dead, without a blow
Made foolish *Ishbosheth*[5] the Crown forgo;
Who banisht *David* did from *Hebron* bring,
And, with a General shout, proclaim'd him King: 60
Those very *Jews* who at their very best
Their Humour more than Loyalty exprest,
Now wondred why so long they had obey'd
An Idol-Monarch which their hands had made;
Thought they might ruine him they could create   65

---

[5] Richard Cromwell. "*Saul*" is of course Oliver Cromwell.

Or melt him to that Golden Calf, a State.
But these were random Bolts: No form'd Design
Nor Interest made the Factious Croud to join:
The sober part of *Israel*, free from stain,
Well knew the value of a peaceful reign;   10
And, looking backward with a wise afright,
Saw Seams of wounds, dishonest to the sight:
In contemplation of whose ugly Scars,
They curst the memory of Civil Wars.
The moderate sort of Men, thus qualifi'd,   15
Inclin'd the Ballance to the better side;
And *David's* mildness manag'd it so well,
The bad found no occasion to Rebel.
But, when to Sin our byast Nature leans,
The careful Devil is still at hand with means;   80
And providently Pimps for ill desires:
The Good Old Cause, reviv'd, a Plot requires,
Plots, true or false, are necessary things,
To raise up Common-wealths and ruin Kings.
    Th' inhabitants of old *Jerusalem*,   85
Were *Jebusites*;[6] the Town so call'd from them;
And their's the Native right——
But when the chosen People grew more strong,
The rightful cause at length became the wrong;
And every loss the men of *Jebus* bore,   90
They still were thought God's enemies the more.
Thus, worn and weaken'd, well or ill content,
Submit they must to *David's* Government:
Impoverish't and depriv'd of all Command,
Their Taxes doubled as they lost their Land;   95
And, what was harder yet to flesh and blood,
Their Gods disgrac'd, and burnt like common Wood.
This set the Heathen Priesthood in a flame,
For Priests of all Religions are the same:
Of whatsoe'er descent their Godhead be,   100
Stock, Stone, or other homely Pedigree,
In his defence his Servants are as bold,
As if he had been born of beaten Gold.
The *Jewish Rabbins*, though their Enemies,
In this conclude them honest men and wise: 105
For 'twas their duty, all the Learned think,
T' espouse his Cause by whom they eat and drink.
From hence began that Plot,[7] the Nations Curse,
Bad in itself, but represented worse,
Rais'd in extremes, and in extremes decri'd,   110
With Oaths affirm'd, with dying Vows deni'd,

---

[6] The Catholics.
[7] The Popish Plot.

Not weigh'd or winnow'd by the Multitude,
But swallow'd in the Mass, unchewed and crude.
Some Truth there was, but dashed and brew'd with Lies;
To please the Fools, and puzzle all the Wise.   115
Succeeding Times did equal Folly call
Believing nothing or believing all.
The *Egyptian* Rites the *Jebusites* embrac'd,
Where Gods were recommended by their taste.
Such sav'ry Deities must needs be good   120
As serv'd at once for Worship and for Food.
By force they could not Introduce these Gods,
For Ten to One in former days was odds.
So Fraud was us'd, (the Sacrificers Trade,)
Fools are more hard to Conquer than Persuade.   125
Their busie Teachers mingled with the *Jews*
And rak'd for Converts even the Court and Stews:
Which *Hebrew* Priests the more unkindly took,
Because the Fleece accompanies the Flock.
Some thought they God's Anointed meant to slay   130
By Guns, invented since full many a day:
Our Author swears it not; but who can know
How far the Devil and *Jebusites* may go?
This Plot, which fail'd for want of common Sense,
Had yet a deep and dangerous Consequence;   135
For as, when raging Fevers boil the Blood
The standing Lake soon floats into a Floud;
And ev'ry hostile Humour which before
Slept quiet in its Channels bubbles o're:
So, several Factions from this first Ferment   140
Work up to Foam, and threat the Government.
Some by their Friends, more by themselves thought wise,
Oppos'd the Pow'r to which they could not rise.
Some had in Courts been Great and, thrown from thence,
Like Fiends were hardened in Impenitence.   145
Some, by their Monarch's fatal mercy grown,
From Pardon'd Rebels, Kinsmen to the Throne
Were raised in Pow'r and Publick Office high;
Strong Bands, if Bands ungrateful men coud tie.
Of these the false *Achitophel*[8] was first,   150
A Name to all succeeding Ages curst.
For close Designs and crooked Counsels fit,
Sagacious, Bold, and Turbulent of wit,
Restless, unfixt in Principles and Place,
In Pow'r unpleased, impatient of Disgrace;   155
A fiery Soul, which working out its way, ⎫
Fretted the Pigmy Body to decay: ⎬
And o'r informed the Tenement of Clay. ⎭

---

[8] The first Earl of Shaftesbury.

A daring Pilot in extremity;
Pleas'd with the Danger, when the Waves went high   160
He sought the Storms; but, for a Calm unfit,
Would Steer too nigh the Sands to boast his Wit.
Great Wits are sure to Madness near alli'd
And thin Partitions do their Bounds divide;
Else, why should he, with Wealth and Honour blest,   165
Refuse his Age the needful hours of Rest?
Punish a Body which he coud not please,
Bankrupt of Life, yet Prodigal of Ease?
And all to leave what with his Toil he won
To that unfeather'd two-legg'd thing, a Son: 170
Got, while his Soul did huddled Notions trie;
And born a shapeless Lump, like Anarchy.
In Friendship false, implacable in Hate,
Resolv'd to Ruine or to Rule the State:
To Compass this the Triple Bond he broke; ⎱   175
The Pillars of the Publick Safety shook, ⎰
And fitted *Israel* for a Foreign Yoke; ⎰
Then, seiz'd with Fear, yet still affecting Fame,
Usurp'd a Patriot's All-attoning Name.
So easie still it proves in Factious Times   180
With publick Zeal to cancel private Crimes:
How safe is Treason and how sacred ill,
Where none can sin against the Peoples Will,
Where Crouds can wink; and no offence be known,
Since in anothers guilt they find their own.   185
Yet, Fame deserv'd, no Enemy can grudge;
The Statesman we abhor, but praise the Judge.
In *Israels* courts ne'er sat an *Abbethdin*[9]
With more discerning Eyes or Hands more clean,
Unbrib'd, unsought, the Wretched to redress;   190
Swift of Dispatch and easie of Access.
Oh, had he been content to serve the Crown
With Vertues onely proper to the Gown,
Or had the rankness of the Soil been freed
From Cockle that opprest the Noble Seed,   195
David for him his tuneful Harp had strung,
And Heav'n had wanted one Immortal Song.
But wild Ambitión loves to slide, not stand,
And Fortunes Ice prefers to Vertues Land.
Achitophel, grown weary to possess   200
A lawful Fame, and lazie Happiness,
Disdain'd the Golden Fruit to gather free
And lent the Crowd his Arm to shake the Tree.
Now, manifest of Crimes, contriv'd long since,
He stood at bold Defiance with his Prince: 205

---

[9] Lord Chancellor.

Held up the Buckler of the Peoples Cause
Against the Crown; and sculk'd behind the Laws.
The wish'd occasion of the Plot he takes;
Some Circumstances finds, but more he makes.
By buzzing Emissaries, fills the ears   210
Of listening Crouds, with Jealousies and Fears
Of Arbitrary Counsels brought to light,
And proves the King himself a *Jebusite*.
Weak Arguments! which yet he knew full well,
Were strong with People easie to Rebel.   215
For, govern'd by the *Moon*, the giddy *Jews*
Tread the same Track when she the Prime renews:
And once in twenty Years, their Scribes record,
By natural Instinct they change their Lord.
Achitophel still wants a Chief, and none   220
Was found so fit as Warlike *Absalon*:
Not, that he wish'd his Greatness to create,
(For Politicians neither love nor hate:)
But, for he knew his Title not allow'd,
Would keep him still depending on the Croud,   225
That Kingly pow'r, thus ebbing out, might be
Drawn to the Dregs of a Democracie.
Him he attempts with studied Arts to please
And sheds his Venome in such words as these.
  Auspicious Prince! at whose Nativity   230
Some Royal Planet rul'd the Southern Sky;
Thy longing Countries Darling and Desire,
Their cloudy Pillar, and their guardian Fire,
Their second *Moses*, whose extended Wand
Divides the Seas and shows the promis'd Land,   235
Whose dawning Day, in every distant Age,
Has exercised the Sacred Prophets rage,
The Peoples Pray'r, the glad Diviners Theam,
The Young mens Vision and the Old mens Dream!
Thee, *Saviour*, Thee the Nations Vows confess;   240
And, never satisfi'd with seeing, bless:
Swift, unbespoken Pomps, thy steps proclaim,
And stammering Babes are taught to lisp thy Name.
How long wilt thou the general Joy detain;
Starve, and defraud the People of thy Reign?   245
Content ingloriously to pass thy days,
Like one of Vertues Fools that Feeds on Praise;
Till thy fresh Glories, which now shine so bright,
Grow Stale and Tarnish with our dayly sight.
Believe me, Royal Youth, thy Fruit must be   250
Or gather'd Ripe, or rot upon the Tree.
Heav'n has to all allotted, soon or late,
Some lucky Revolution of their Fate:

Whose Motions, if we watch and guide with Skill,
(For humane Good depends on humane Will,)   255
Our Fortune rolls as from a smooth Descent
And, from the first impression, takes the Bent;
But, if unseiz'd, she glides away like wind;
And leaves repenting Folly far behind.
Now, now she meets you with a glorious prize   260
And spreads her Locks before her as she flies.
Had thus Old *David*, from whose Loins you spring,
Not dar'd, when Fortune call'd him, to be King,
At *Gath* an Exile he might still remain,
And Heavens Anointing Oil had been in vain.   265
Let his successful Youth your hopes engage,
But shun th' example of Declining Age.
Behold him setting in his Western Skies,
The Shadows lengthening as the Vapours rise.
He is not now, as when, on *Jordan's* Sand,   270
The Joyful People throng'd to see him Land,
Cov'ring the *Beach* and blackning all the *Strand*:
But like the Prince of Angels, from his height,
Comes tumbling downward with diminish'd light:
Betray'd by one poor Plot to publick Scorn,   275
(Our onely blessing since his curst Return,)
Those heaps of People which one Sheaf did bind,
Blown off and scatter'd by a puff of Wind.
What strength can he to your Designs oppose,
Naked of Friends, and round beset with Foes?   280
If *Pharaoh's*[10] doubtful succour he should use,
A Foreign Aid would more incense the *Jews*:
Proud *Egypt* woud dissembled Friendship bring;
Foment the War, but not support the King:
Nor woud the Royal Party e'r unite   285
With *Pharaoh's* arms t' assist the *Jebusite*;
Or if they shoud, their Interest soon would break,
And, with such odious Aid, make *David* weak.
All sorts of men, by my successful Arts
Abhorring Kings, estrange their altered Hearts   290
From *David's* Rule: And 'tis the general Cry,
Religion, Common-wealth, and Liberty.
If you, as Champion of the Publique Good,
Add to their Arms a Chief of Royal Blood;
What may not *Israel* hope, and what Applause   295
Might such a General gain by such a Cause?
Not barren Praise alone, that Gaudy Flow'r,
Fair onely to the sight, but solid Pow'r:
And Nobler is a limited Command,

---

[10] Louis XIV.

Giv'n by the Love of all your Native Land,   300
Than a Successive Title, Long, and Dark,
Drawn from the Mouldy Rolls of *Noah's* ark.
  What cannot Praise effect in Mighty Minds,
When Flattery Sooths and when Ambition Blinds!
Desire of Pow'r, on Earth a Vitious Weed,   305
Yet, sprung from High is of Cœlestial Seed;
In God 'tis Glory: And when Men Aspire,
'Tis but a Spark too much of Heavenly Fire.
Th' Ambitious Youth, too Covetous of Fame,
Too full of Angels Metal in his Frame,   310
Unwarily was led from Vertues ways,
Made Drunk with Honour, and debauch'd with Praise.
Half loath and half consenting to the Ill,
(For Loyal Blood within him strugled still,)
He thus repli'd—And what Pretence have I   315
To take up Arms for Publick Liberty?
My Father Governs with unquestion'd Right;
The Faiths Defender and Mankinds Delight,
Good, Gracious, Just, observant of the Laws;
And Heav'n by Wonders has espous'd his Cause.   320
Whom has he Wrong'd in all his Peaceful Reign?
Who sues for Justice to his Throne in Vain?
What Millions has he pardoned of his Foes
Whom Just Revenge did to his Wrath expose?
Mild, Easie, Humble, Studious of our Good,   325
Enclin'd to Mercy, and averse from Blood.
If Mildness Ill with Stubborn *Israel* Suit,
His Crime is God's beloved Attribute.
What could he gain, his People to Betray
Or change his Right, for Arbitrary Sway?   330
Let Haughty *Pharaoh* Curse with such a Reign
His Fruitful *Nile*, and Yoak a Servile Train.
If *David's* Rule *Jerusalem* Displease,
The *Dog-star* heats their Brains to this Disease.
Why then should I, Encouraging the Bad,   335
Turn Rebel and run Popularly Mad?
Were he a Tyrant who, by Lawless Might,
Opprest the *Jews* and rais'd the *Jebusite*,
Well might I Mourn; but Nature's holy Bands
Would Curb my Spirits, and Restrain my Hands;   340
The People might assert their Liberty;
But what was Right in them, were Crime in me.
His Favour leaves me nothing to require;
Prevents my Wishes and out-runs Desire.
What more can I expect while *David* lives?   345
All but his Kingly Diadem he gives:
And that: But there he paus'd; then Sighing, said,

Is Justly destin'd for a Worthier head.
For when my Father from his Toyls shall Rest
And late Augment the Number of the Blest: 350
His Lawful Issue shall the Throne ascend,
Or the *Collat'ral* Line, where that shall end.
His Brother, though Opprest with Vulgar Spight,
Yet Dauntless and Secure of Native Right,
Of every Royal Vertue stands possest;   355
Still Dear to all the Bravest and the Best.
His Courage Foes, his Friends his Truth Proclaim;
His Loyalty the King, the World his Fame.
His Mercy ev'n th' Offending Croud will find,
For sure he comes of a Forgiving Kind.   360
Why shoud I then Repine at Heavens Decree
Which gives me no Pretence to Royalty?
Yet oh that Fate, Propitiously Inclin'd,
Had rais'd my Birth, or had debas'd my Mind;
To my large Soul, not all her Treasure lent,   365
And then betrai'd it to a mean Descent.
I find, I find my mounting Spirits Bold,
And *David's* part disdains my Mothers Mold.
Why am I scanted by a Niggard Birth?
My soul Disclaims the Kindred of her Earth: 370
And, made for Empire, Whispers me within;
Desire of Greatness is a God-like Sin.
   Him Staggering so when Hells dire Agent found,
While fainting Vertue scarce maintain'd her Ground,
He pours fresh Forces in, and thus Replies: 375
   Th' eternal God, Supreamly Good and Wise,
Imparts not these Prodigious Gifts in vain;
What Wonders are Reserv'd to bless your Reign?
Against your will your Arguments have shown,
Such Vertue's only giv'n to guide a Throne.   380
Not that your Father's Mildness I contemn,
But manly Force becomes the Diadem.
'Tis true he grants the People all they crave;
And more perhaps than Subjects ought to have:
For Lavish Grants suppose a Monarch tame   385
And more his Goodness than his Wit proclaim.
But when should People strive their Bonds to break,
If not when Kings are Negligent or Weak?
Let him give on till he can give no more,
The thrifty Sanhedrin shall keep him poor: 390
And every Sheckle which he can receive
Shall cost a Limb of his Prerogative.
To ply him with new Plots shall be my care;
Or plunge him deep in some Expensive War;
Which, when his Treasure can no more supply,   395

He must, with the Remains of Kingship, buy.
His faithful Friends our Jealousies and Fears
Call *Jebusites*; and *Pharaoh's* Pensioners,
Whom, when our Fury from his Aid has torn,
He shall be naked left to publick Scorn.   400
The next Successor, whom I fear and hate,
My Arts have made obnoxious to the State;
Turn'd all his Vertues to his Overthrow,
And gain'd our Elders to pronounce a Foe.
His Right, for Sums of necessary Gold,   405
Shall first be Pawn'd, and afterwards be Sold;
Till time shall Ever-wanting *David* draw,
To pass your doubtful Title into Law.
If not; the People have a Right Supreme
To make their Kings; for Kings are made for them.   410
All Empire is no more than Pow'r in Trust,
Which, when resum'd, can be no longer Just.
Succession, for the general Good design'd,
In its own wrong a Nation cannot bind:
If altering that, the People can relieve,   415
Better one suffer, than a Nation grieve.
The *Jews* well know their pow'r: e'r *Saul*[11] they chose
God was their King, and God they durst Depose.
Urge now your Piety, your Filial Name,
A Father's Right and Fear of future Fame;   420
The Publick Good, that Universal Call,
To which even Heav'n submitted, answers all.
Nor let his Love enchant your generous Mind;
'Tis Natures trick to propagate her Kind.
Our fond Begetters, who would never die,   425
Love but themselves in their Posterity.
Or let his Kindness by th' Effects be tried
Or let him lay his vain Pretence aside.
God said he loved your Father; coud he bring
A better Proof than to anoint him King?   430
It surely shew'd, He lov'd the Shepherd well
Who gave so fair a Flock as *Israel*.
Would *David* have you thought his Darling Son?
What means he then, to Alienate the Crown?
The name of Godly he may blush to bear: 435
'Tis after Gods own heart to Cheat his Heir.
He to his Brother gives Supreme Command;
To you a Legacie of Barren Land:
Perhaps th' old Harp on which he thrums his Lays:
Or some dull *Hebrew* Ballad in your Praise.   440
Then the next Heir, a Prince, Severe and Wise,

---

[11] Oliver Cromwell.

Already looks on you with Jealous Eyes,
Sees through the thin Disguises of your Arts,
And marks your Progress in the Peoples Hearts.
Though now his mighty Soul its Grief contains; 445
He meditates Revenge who least Complains.
And like a Lion, Slumb'ring in the way,
Or Sleep dissembling, while he waits his Prey,
His fearless Foes within his Distance draws,
Constrains his Roaring, and Contracts his Paws: 450
Till at the last, his time for Fury found,
He shoots with sudden Vengeance from the Ground:
The Prostrate Vulgar, passes o'r and Spares;
But with a Lordly Rage, his Hunters tears;
Your Case no tame Expedients will afford; 455
Resolve on Death, or Conquest by the Sword,
Which for no less a Stake than Life, you Draw,
And Self-defence is Natures Eldest Law.
Leave the warm People no Considering time;
For then Rebellion may be thought a Crime. 460
Prevail your self of what Occasion gives,
But trie your Title while your Father lives;
And, that your Arms may have a fair Pretence,
Proclaim, you take them in the King's Defence;
Whose Sacred Life each minute woud Expose, 465
To Plots, from seeming Friends and secret Foes.
And who can sound the depth of *David's* Soul?
Perhaps his fear, his kindness may Controul.
He fears his Brother, though he loves his Son,
For plighted Vows too late to be undone. 470
If so, by Force he wishes to be gain'd,
Like Womens Leachery to seem Constrain'd:
Doubt not; but, when he most affects the Frown,
Commit a pleasing Rape upon the Crown.
Secure his Person to secure your Cause; 475
They who possess the Prince, possess the Laws.
   He said, And this Advice above the rest
With *Absalon's* Mild Nature suited best;
Unblamed of Life (Ambition set aside,)
Not stain'd with Cruelty, nor puft with pride. 480
How happy had he been, if Destiny
Had higher placed his Birth, or not so high!
His Kingly Vertues might have claim'd a Throne
And blest all other Countries but his own:
But charming Greatness, since so few refuse; 485
'Tis Juster to Lament him, than Accuse.
Strong were his hopes a Rival to remove,
With Blandishments to gain the publick Love,
To Head the Faction while their Zeal was hot,

And Popularly Prosecute the Plot. 490
To farther this, *Achitophel* Unites
The Malecontents of all the *Israelites:*
Whose differing Parties he could wisely Join
For several Ends, to serve the same Design.
The Best, and of the Princes some were such, 495
Who thought the pow'r of Monarchy too much:
Mistaken Men, and Patriots in their Hearts;
Not Wicked, but seduc'd by Impious Arts.
By these the Springs of Property were bent,
And wound so high, they Crack'd the Government. 500
The next for Interest sought t' embroil the State,
To sell their Duty at a dearer rate;
And make their *Jewish* Markets of the Throne;
Pretending Publick Good, to serve their own.
Others thought Kings an useless heavy Load, 505
Who Cost too much, and did too little Good.
These were for laying Honest *David* by
On Principles of pure good Husbandry.
With them join'd all th' Haranguers of the Throng
That thought to get Preferment by the Tongue. 510
Who follow next, a double danger bring,
Not onely hating *David*, but the King;
The *Solymæan* Rout;[12] well Vers'd of old
In Godly Faction, and in Treason bold;
Cowring and Quaking at a Conqu'ror's Sword, 515
But Lofty to a Lawful Prince Restored;
Saw with Disdain an *Ethnick* Plot begun
And Scorned by *Jebusites* to be Out-done.
Hot *Levites* Headed these; who pul'd before
From th' *Ark*, which in the Judges days they bore, 520
Resum'd their Cant, and with a Zealous Crie
Pursu'd their old belov'd Theocracie.
Where Sanhedrin and Priest enslav'd the Nation
And justifi'd their Spoils by Inspiration:
For who so fit for Reign as *Aaron's* Race, 525
If once Dominion they could found in Grace?
These led the Pack; though not of surest scent,
Yet deepest mouth'd against the Government.
A numerous Host of dreaming Saints succeed;
Of the true old Enthusiastick Breed: 530
'Gainst Form and Order they their Pow'r imploy;
Nothing to Build, and all things to Destroy.
But far more numerous was the Herd of such,
Who think too little, and who talk too much.
These, out of meer instinct, they knew not why, 535

---

[12] London rebels.

Adored their Fathers' God, and Property:
And, by the same blind Benefit of Fate,
The Devil and the *Jebusite* did hate:
Born to be sav'd, even in their own despight;   540
Because they could not help believing right.
Such were the Tools; but a whole Hydra more
Remains, of sprouting heads too long to score.
Some of their Chiefs were Princes of the Land;
In the first Rank of these did *Zimri*[13] stand: 545
A man so various, that he seem'd to be
Not one, but all Mankind's Epitome.
Stiff in Opinions, always in the wrong;
Was Every thing by starts, and Nothing long:
But, in the course of one revolving Moon,   550
Was Chymist, Fidler, States-man, and Buffoon;
Then all for Women, Painting, Rhiming, Drinking,
Besides ten thousand Freaks that died in thinking.
Blest Madman, who coud every hour employ,
With something New to wish, or to enjoy!
Railing and praising were his usual Theams;   555
And both (to shew his Judgment) in Extreams:
So over Violent, or over Civil,
That every Man, with him, was God or Devil.
In squandring Wealth was his peculiar Art:
Nothing went unrewarded, but Desert.   560
Begger'd by fools, whom still he found too late:
He had his Jest, and they had his Estate.
He laugh'd himself from Court; then sought Relief
By forming Parties, but could ne'r be Chief:
For, spight of him, the weight of Business fell   565
On *Absolon* and wise *Achitophel*:
Thus wicked but in Will, of Means bereft,
He left not Faction, but of that was left.
   Titles and Names 'twere tedious to Reherse
Of Lords, below the Dignity of Verse.   570
Wits, Warriors, Commonwealths-men were the best:
Kind Husbands and meer Nobles all the rest
And, therefore in the name of Dulness, be
The well-hung *Balaam*[14] and cold *Caleb*[15] free;
And Canting *Nadab*[16] let Oblivion damn,   575
Who made new Porridge for the Paschal Lamb.
Let Friendships holy Band some Names assure,
Some their own Worth, and some let Scorn secure.
Nor shall the Rascal Rabble here have Place,

[13] The Duke of Buckingham.
[14] The Earl of Huntingdon.
[15] Lord Grey.
[16] Lord Howard of Escrick.

Whom Kings no Titles gave, and God no Grace: 580
Not Bull-fac'd *Jonas*, who coud Statutes draw
To mean Rebellion, and make Treason Law.
But he, though bad, is follow'd by a worse,
The Wretch, who Heav'ns Anointed dar'd to Curse.
Shimei,[17] whose Youth did early Promise bring   585
Of Zeal to God, and Hatred to his King;
Did wisely from Expensive Sins refrain,
And never broke the Sabbath, but for Gain:
Nor ever was he known an Oath to vent,
Or Curse, unless against the Government.   590
Thus, heaping Wealth, by the most ready way
Among the *Jews*, which was to Cheat and Pray;
The City, to reward his pious Hate
Against his Master, chose him Magistrate:
His Hand a Vare of Justice did uphold;   595
His Neck was loaded with a Chain of Gold.
During his Office, Treason was no Crime.
The Sons of *Belial* had a Glorious Time:
For *Shimei*, though not prodigal of pelf,
Yet lov'd his wicked Neighbour as himself: 600
When two or three were gather'd to declaim
Against the Monarch of *Jerusalem*,
Shimei was always in the midst of them.
And, if they Curst the King when he was by,
Woud rather Curse, than break good Company.   605
If any durst his Factious Friends accuse,
He pact a jury of dissenting *Jews*:
Whose fellow-feeling, in the godly Cause,
Would free the suff'ring Saint from Humane Laws.
For Laws are onely made to Punish those   610
Who serve the King, and to protect his Foes.
If any leisure time he had from Pow'r,
(Because 'tis Sin to misimploy an hour;)
His bus'ness was by Writing to persuade
That kings were Useless, and a Clog to Trade: 615
And that his noble Stile he might refine,
No *Rechabite* more shund the fumes of Wine.
Chaste were his Cellars; and his Shrieval Board
The Grossness of a City Feast abhor'd:
His Cooks, with long disuse, their Trade forgot;   620
Cool was his Kitchin, though his Brains were hot.
Such frugal Vertue Malice may accuse;
But sure 'twas necessary to the *Jews*:
For Towns once burnt, such Magistrates require
As dare not tempt Gods Providence by Fire.   625

---

[17] Slingsley Bethel, one of the sheriffs of London.

With Spiritual Food he fed his Servants well,
But free from Flesh that made the *Jews* rebel:
And *Moses's* Laws he held in more account,
For forty days of Fasting in the Mount.
To speak the rest, who better are forgot, 630
Would tire a well-breath'd Witness of the Plot:
Yet, *Corah*,[18] thou shalt from Oblivion pass;
Erect thy self thou Monumental Brass:
High as the Serpent of thy Metal made,
While Nations stand secure beneath thy shade. 635
What though his Birth were base, yet Comets rise
From Earthy Vapours, e'r they shine in Skies.
Prodigious Actions may as well be done
By Weaver's issue as by Prince's son.
This Arch-Attestor for the Publick Good 640
By that one Deed enobles all his Bloud.
Who'ever ask'd the Witnesses high race
Whose Oath with Martyrdom did *Stephen* grace?
Ours was a *Levite*, and as times went then,
His tribe were God-almighties Gentlemen. 645
Sunk were his Eyes, his Voice was harsh and loud,
Sure signs he neither Cholerick was, nor Proud:
His long Chin prov'd his Wit; his Saint-like Grace
A Church Vermilion, and a *Moses's* Face.
His Memory, miraculously great, 650
Coud Plots, exceeding mans belief, repeat;
Which, therefore cannot be accounted Lies,
For humane Wit coud never such devise.
Some future Truths are mingled in his Book;
But where the Witness fail'd, the Prophet spoke: 655
Some things like Visionary flights appear;
The Spirit caught him up, the Lord knows where:
And gave him his *Rabinical* degree,
Unknown to Foreign University.
His Judgment yet his Mem'ry did excel, 660
Which piec'd his wondrous Evidence so well:
And suited to the temper of the Times;
Then groaning under *Jebusitick* Crimes.
Let *Israels* foes suspect his Heav'nly call,
And rashly judge his Writ Apocryphal; 665
Our Laws for such affronts have Forfeits made:
He takes his Life, who takes away his Trade.
Were I myself in Witness *Corah's* place,
The Wretch who did me such a dire disgrace
Should whet my memory, though once forgot, 670
To make him an Appendix of my Plot.

---

[18] Titus Oates.

His Zeal to Heav'n, made him his Prince despise,
And load his Person with indignities:
But Zeal peculiar priviledge affords,
Indulging latitude to deeds and words: 675
And *Corah* might for *Agag's* murther[19] call,
In terms as course as *Samuel* us'd 'to *Saul*.
What others in his Evidence did join,
(The best that coud be had for love or coin,)
In *Corah's* own predicament will fall   680
For *Witness* is a Common Name to all.
    Surrounded thus with Friends of every sort,
Deluded *Absolom* forsakes the Court:
Impatient of high hopes, urg'd with renown,
And Fir'd with near possession of a Crown.   685
The admiring Croud are dazled with surprize
And on his goodly person feed their eyes:
His joy conceal'd, he sets himself to show;
On each side bowing popularly low:
His looks, his gestures, and his words he frames   690
And with familiar ease repeats their Names.
Thus, form'd by Nature, furnished out with Arts,
He glides unfelt into their secret hearts:
Then with a kind compassionating look,
And sighs, bespeaking pity e'r he spoke,   695
Few words he said, but easie those and fit,
More slow than Hybla drops, and far more sweet.
    I mourn, my Country-men, your lost Estate,
Though far unable to prevent your Fate:
Behold a Banish'd man, for your dear cause   700
Expos'd a prey to Arbitrary Laws!
Yet oh! that I alone coud be undone,
Cut off from Empire, and no more a Son!
Now all your Liberties a spoil are made;
Egypt[20] and *Tyrus*[21] intercept your Trade,   705
And *Jebusites* your Sacred Rites invade.
My Father, whom with reverence yet I name,
Charm'd into Ease, is 'careless of his Fame:
And, brib'd with petty sums of Foreign Gold,
Is grown in *Bathsheba's*[22] Embraces old: 710
Exalts his Enemies, his Friends destroys,
And all his pow'r against himself imploys.
He gives, and let him give my right away;
But why should he his own and yours betray?
He onely, he can make the Nation bleed,   715

---

[19] The murder of Sir Edmund Bury Godfrey, October, 1678.
[20] France.
[21] Holland.
[22] The Duchess of Portsmouth.

And he alone from my revenge is freed.
Take then my tears (with that he wiped his Eyes)
'Tis all the Aid my present pow'r supplies:
No Court-Informer can these Arms accuse;
These Arms may Sons against their Fathers use;   720
And, 'tis my wish, the next Successor's reign
May make no other *Israelite* complain.
   Youth, Beauty, Graceful Action seldom fail:
But Common Interest always will prevail:
And pity never Ceases to be shown   725
To him, who makes the Peoples wrongs his own.
The Croud, (that still believe their Kings oppress,)
With lifted hands their young *Messiah* bless:
Who now begins his Progress to ordain
With Chariots, Horsemen, and a num'rous train;   730
From East to West his Glories he displays:
And, like the Sun, the Promis'd Land surveys.
Fame runs before him as the Morning-Star,
And shouts of Joy salute him from afar:
Each house receives him as a Guardian God;   735
And Consecrates the Place of his abode:
But hospitable Treats did most commend
Wise *Issachar*, his wealthy Western Friend.
This moving Court that caught the Peoples Eyes,
And seem'd but Pomp, did other Ends disguise: 740
Achitophel had form'd it, with intent
To sound the depths, and fathom where it went,
The Peoples hearts distinguish Friends from Foes;
And trie their strength before they came to Blows.
Yet all was colour'd with a smooth pretence   745
Of specious love, and duty to their Prince.
Religion, and Redress of Grievances,
Two names, that always cheat and always please,
Are often urg'd; and good King *David's* life
Endanger'd by a Brother and a Wife.   750
Thus, in a Pageant Shew, a Plot is made;
And Peace it self is War in Masquerade.
Oh foolish *Israel*! never warn'd by Ill:
Still the same Bait, and circumvented still!
Did ever men forsake their present ease,   755
In midst of health imagine a Disease;
Take pains Contingent mischiefs to foresee,
Make Heirs for Monarchs, and for God decree?
What shall we think! Can People give away
Both for themselves and Sons their Native sway?   760
Then they are left Defenceless, to the Sword
Of each unbounded, Arbitrary Lord:
And Laws are vain, by which we Right enjoy,

If Kings unquestion'd can those Laws destroy.
Yet if the Croud be Judge of Fit and Just,   765
And Kings are onely Officers in Trust,
Then this resuming Cov'nant was declar'd
When Kings were made, or is for ever bar'd:
If those who gave the Scepter, coud not tie
By their own Deed their own Posterity,   770
How then coud *Adam* bind his future Race?
How coud his Forfeit on Mankind take place?
Or how coud heavenly Justice damn us all
Who ne'r consented to our Fathers Fall?
Then Kings are Slaves to those whom they command,   775
And Tenants to their Peoples pleasure stand.
Add that the Pow'r, for Property allow'd,
Is mischievously seated in the Croud;
For who can be secure of private Right,
If Sovereign Sway may be dissolv'd by Might?   780
Nor is the Peoples Judgment always true:
The Most may err as grosly as the Few.
And faultless Kings run down, by Common Cry,
For Vice, Oppression, and for Tyranny.
What Standard is there in a fickle rout,   785
Which, flowing to the Mark, runs faster out?
Nor onely crouds, but Sanhedrins may be
Infected with this publick Lunacy:
And Share the madness of Rebellious Times,
To Murther Monarchs for Imagin'd crimes.   790
If they may Give and Take when e'r they please,
Not Kings alone, (the Godheads Images,)
But Government it self at length must fall
To Natures state, where all have Right to all.
Yet, grant our Lords the People, Kings can make,   795
What prudent men a setled Throne woud shake?
For whatsoe'r their Sufferings were before,
That Change they Covet makes them suffer more.
All other Errors but disturb a State;
But Innovation is the Blow of Fate.   800
If ancient Fabricks nod, and threat to fall,
To Patch the Flaws, and Buttress up the Wall,
Thus far 'tis Duty; but here fix the Mark:
For all beyond it is to touch our Ark.
To change Foundations, cast the Frame anew,   805
Is work for Rebels who base Ends pursue:
At once Divine and Humane Laws controul,
And mend the Parts by ruine of the Whole.
The tamp'ring World is subject to this Curse,
To Physick their Disease into a Worse.   810
    Now, what Relief can Righteous *David* bring?

How Fatal 'tis to be too good a King!
Friends he has few, so high the madness grows;
Who dare be such, must be the People's Foes:
Yet some there were ev'n in the worst of days; 815
Some let me name, and Naming is to praise.
   In this short File *Barzillai*[23] first appears;
Barzillai crown'd with Honour and with Years:
Long since, the rising Rebels he withstood
In Regions Waste, beyond the *Jordans* Flood: 820
Unfortunately Brave to buoy the State;
But sinking underneath his Master's Fate:
In Exile with his God-like Prince he Mourn'd,
For him he Suffer'd, and with him Return'd.
The Court he practis'd, not the Courtier's Art: 825
Large was his Wealth, but larger was his Heart:
Which, well the Noblest Objects knew to chuse,
The Fighting Warriour, and Recording Muse.
His Bed coud once a Fruitful Issue boast:
Now more than half a Father's Name is lost. 830
His Eldest Hope, with every Grace adorn'd,
By me (so Heav'n will have it) always Mourn'd
And always honour'd, snatch'd in manhoods prime
B' unequal Fates and Providences crime:
Yet not before the Goal of Honour won, 835
All Parts fulfill'd of Subject and of Son;
Swift was the Race, but short the Time to run.
Oh Narrow Circle, but of Pow'r Divine,
Scanted in Space, but perfect in thy Line!
By Sea, by Land, thy Matchless Worth was known; 840
Arms thy Delight, and War was all thy Own:
Thy force, Infus'd, the fainting *Tyrians* prop'd;
And haughty *Pharaoh* found his Fortune stop'd.
Oh Ancient Honour, Oh unconquered Hand,
Whom Foes unpunish'd never coud withstand! 845
But *Israel* was unworthy of thy Name:
Short is the date of all Immoderate Fame.
It looks as Heav'n our Ruine had design'd,
And durst not trust thy Fortune and thy Mind.
Now, free from Earth, thy disencumbred Soul 850
Mounts up, and leaves behind the Clouds and Starry Pole:
From thence thy kindred Legions maist thou bring,
To aid the Guardian Angel of thy King.
Here stop my Muse, here cease thy painful flight;
No pinions can pursue Immortal height: 855
Tell good *Barzillai* thou canst sing no more,
And tell thy Soul she should have fled before;
Or fled she with his life, and left this Verse

---

[23] The Duke of Ormond.

To hang on her departed Patron's Herse?
Now take thy steepy flight from Heav'n, and see   860
If thou canst find on Earth another *He*;
Another he would be too hard to find;
See then whom thou canst see not far behind.
Zadock[24] the priest, whom, shunning Pow'r and Place,
His lowly mind advanc'd to *David's* Grace: 865
With him the *Sagan* of *Jerusalem*,[25]
Of hospitable Soul and noble Stem;
Him of the Western dome, whose weighty sense
Flows in fit words and heavenly eloquence.
The Prophets Sons, by such Example led,   870
To Learning and to Loyalty were bred:
For *Colleges* on bounteous Kings depend,
And never Rebel was to Arts a Friend.
To these succeed the Pillars of the Laws,
Who best coud plead, and best can judge a Cause.   875
Next them a train of Loyal Peers ascend:
Sharp judging *Adriel*,[26] the Muses Friend,
Himself a Muse:—In Sanhedrins debate
True to his Prince, but not a Slave of State.
Whom *David's* love with Honours did adorn,   880
That from his disobedient Son were torn.
Jotham[27] of piercing Wit and pregnant Thought,
Endew'd by nature and by learning taught
To move Assemblies, who but onely tri'd
The worse a while, then chose the better side;   885
Nor chose alone, but turned the Balance too;
So much the weight of one brave man can do.
Hushai[28] the friend of *David* in distress,
In publick storms of manly stedfastness;
By Foreign Treaties he inform'd his Youth;   890
And join'd Experience to his Native Truth.
His frugal care suppli'd the wanting Throne;
Frugal for that, but bounteous of his own:
'Tis easie Conduct when Exchequers flow;
But hard the task to manage well the low: 895
For Sovereign Power is too deprest or high,
When Kings are forced to sell, or Crouds to buy.
Indulge one labour more, my weary Muse,
For *Amiel*;[29] who can *Amiel's* praise refuse?
Of ancient race by birth, but nobler yet   900
In his own worth, and without Title great:

---

[24] Archbishop Sancroft.
[25] The Bishop of London.
[26] The Earl of Mulgrave.
[27] The Marquis of Halifax.
[28] Laurence Hyde, Earl of Rochester.
[29] Edward Seymour.

The Sanhedrin long time as Chief he rul'd,
Their Reason guided, and their Passion coold:
So dextrous was he in the Crown's defence,
So form'd to speak a Loyal Nations Sense,   905
That, as their Band was *Israels* Tribes in small,
So fit was he to represent them all.
Now rasher Charioteers the Seat ascend,
Whose loose Carriers his steady Skill commend:
They, like th' unequal Ruler of the Day,   910
Misguide the Seasons, and mistake the Way;
While he withdrawn at their mad Labour smiles
And safe enjoys the Sabbath of his Toils.
    These were the chief; a small but faithful Band
Of Worthies in the Breach who dar'd to stand   915
And tempt th' united Fury of the Land.
With grief they view'd such powerful Engines bent
To batter down the lawful Government.
A numerous Faction with pretended frights,
In Sanhedrins to plume the Regal Rights.   920
The true Successor from the Court removed:
The plot, by hireling Witnesses improv'd.
These Ills they saw, and, as their Duty bound,
They shew'd the King the danger of the Wound:
That no Concessions from the Throne woud please;   925
But Lenitives fomented the Disease;
That *Absalom*, ambitious of the Crown,
Was made the Lure to draw the People down:
That false *Achitophel's* pernitious Hate
Had turn'd the Plot to ruine Church and State;   930
The Council violent, the Rabble worse:
That *Shimei* taught *Jerusalem* to Curse.
    With all these loads of Injuries opprest,
And long revolving in his careful Brest
Th' event of things; at last his patience tir'd,   935
Thus from his Royal Throne, by Heav'n inspir'd,
The God-like *David* spoke; with awful fear
His Train their Maker in their Master hear.
    Thus long have I by Native Mercy sway'd,
My Wrongs dissembl'd, my Revenge delay'd;   940
So willing to forgive th' Offending Age;
So much the Father did the King asswage.
But now so far my Clemency they slight,
Th' Offenders question my Forgiving Right.
That one was made for many, they contend;   945
But 'tis to Rule, for that's a Monarch's End.
They call my tenderness of Blood, my Fear,
Though Manly tempers can the longest bear.
Yet since they will divert my Native course,

'Tis time to show I am not Good by Force.   950
Those heap'd Affronts that haughty Subjects bring,
Are burdens for a Camel, not a King:
Kings are the publick Pillars of the State,
Born to sustain and prop the Nations weight:
If my young *Sampson* will pretend a Call   955
To shake the Column, let him share the Fall:
But oh that yet he woud repent and live!
How easie 'tis for Parents to forgive!
With how few Tears a Pardon might be won
From Nature, pleading for a Darling Son!   960
Poor pitied youth, by my Paternal care,
Rais'd up to all the Height his Frame coud bear:
Had God ordain'd his Fate for Empire born,
He woud have giv'n his Soul another turn:
Gull'd with a Patriot's name, whose Modern sense   965
Is one that woud by Law supplant his Prince:
The Peoples Brave, the Politicians Tool;
Never was Patriot yet, but was a Fool.
Whence comes it that Religion and the Laws
Should more be *Absalon's* than *David's* Cause?   970
His old Instructor, e'r he lost his Place,
Was never thought indu'd with so much Grace.
Good heav'ns, how Faction can a Patriot Paint!
My Rebel ever proves my Peoples Saint:
Woud *They* impose an Heir upon the Throne?   975
Let Sanhedrins be taught to give their Own.
A king's at least a part of Government;
And mine as requisite as their Consent:
Without my leave a future King to choose,
Infers a Right the present to Depose: 980
True, they petition me t' approve their Choice:
But *Esau's* Hands suit ill with *Jacob's* Voice.
My Pious Subjects for my Safety pray,
Which to Secure, they take my Pow'r away.
From Plots and Treasons Heav'n preserve my Years,   985
But save me most from my Petitioners.
Unsatiate as the barren Womb or Grave;
God cannot Grant so much as they can Crave.
What then is left but with a Jealous Eye
To guard the Small remains of Royalty?   990
The Law shall still direct my peaceful Sway,
And the same Law teach Rebels to obey:
Votes shall no more Established Pow'r controul,
Such Votes as make a Part exceed the Whole:
No groundless Clamours shall my Friends remove   995
Nor Crouds have pow'r to Punish e'r they Prove;
For Gods and God-like kings their Care express,

Still to defend their Servants in distress.
Oh that my Pow'r to Saving were confin'd:
Why am I forc'd, like Heav'n, against my mind,   1000
To make Examples of another Kind?
Must I at length the Sword of Justice draw?
Oh curst Effects of necessary Law!
How ill my Fear they by my Mercy scan,
Beware the Fury of a Patient Man.   1005
Law they require, let Law then shew her Face;
They could not be content to look on Grace,
Her hinder parts, but with a daring Eye
To tempt the terror of her Front, and die.
By their own Arts 'tis Righteously decreed,   1010
Those dire Artificers of Death shall bleed.
Against themselves their Witnesses will Swear,
Till, Viper-like, their Mother Plot they tear,
And suck for Nutriment that bloudy gore
Which was their Principle of Life before.   1015
Their *Belial* with their *Belzebub* will fight;
Thus on my Foes, my Foes shall do me Right.
Nor doubt th' event; for Factious crouds engage
In their first Onset, all their Brutal Rage;
Then let 'em take an unresisted Course;   1020
Retire and Traverse, and Delude their Force:
But when they stand all Breathless, urge the fight,
And rise upon 'em with redoubled might:
For Lawful Pow'r is still Superiour found,
When long driv'n back, at length it stands the ground. 1025
    He said. Th' Almighty, nodding, gave consent;
And peals of Thunder shook the Firmament.
Henceforth a Series of new time began,
The mighty Years in long Procession ran:
Once more the God-like *David* was Restor'd,   1030
And willing Nations knew their Lawful Lord.

The Medal. A Satire against Sedition[1]

OF ALL our Antick Sights, and Pageantry
Which *English* Ideots run in crowds to see,
The *Polish Medall* bears the prize alone:
A Monster, more the Favourite of the Town
Than either Fayrs or Theatres have shown.   5

---

[1] Published in March, 1682. Text of first edition. The occasion was the striking of
a medal in the City to commemorate Shaftesbury's acquittal on a charge of high treason.

Never did Art so well with Nature strive;
Nor ever Idol seem'd so much alive:
So like the Man, so golden to the sight,
So base within, so counterfeit and light.
One side is fill'd with Title and with Face;   10
And, lest the King shou'd want a regal Place,
On the reverse, a Tow'r the Town surveys;
O'er which our mounting Sun his beams displays.
The Word, pronounc'd aloud by Shrieval voice,
Lætamur, which, in *Polish*, is *rejoyce*.   15
The Day, Month, Year, to the great Act are join'd:
And a new Canting Holiday design'd.
Five daies he sate, for every cast and look;
Four more than God to finish *Adam* took.
But who can tell what Essence Angels are,   20
Or how long Heav'n was making *Lucifer?*
Oh, cou'd the Style that copy'd every grace,
And plough'd such furrows for an Eunuch face,
Cou'd it have form'd his ever-changing Will,
The various Piece had tir'd the Graver's Skill!   25
A Martial Heroe first, with early care,
Blown, like a Pigmee by the Winds, to war.
A beardless Chief, a Rebel, e'r a Man:
(So young his hatred to his Prince began.)
Next this, (How wildly will Ambition steer!)   30
A Vermin, wriggling in th' Usurper's Ear.
Bart'ring his venal wit for sums of gold
He cast himself into the Saint-like mould;
Groan'd, sigh'd and pray'd, while Godliness was gain;
The lowdest Bagpipe of the squeaking Train.   35
But, as 'tis hard to cheat a Juggler's Eyes,
His open lewdness he cou'd ne'er disguise.
There split the Saint: for Hypocritique Zeal
Allows no Sins but those it can conceal.
Whoring to Scandal gives too large a scope: 40
Saints must not trade; but they may interlope.
Th' ungodly Principle was all the same;
But a gross Cheat betrays his Partner's Game.
Besides, their pace was formal, grave and slack:
His nimble Wit outran the heavy Pack.   45
Yet still he found his Fortune at a stay;
Whole droves of Blockheads choaking up his way;
They took, but not rewarded, his advice;
Villain and Wit exact a double price.
Pow'r was his aym: but, thrown from that pretence,   50
The Wretch turn'd loyal in his own defence;
And Malice reconcil'd him to his Prince.
Him, in the anguish of his Soul he serv'd;

Rewarded faster still than he deserv'd.
Behold him now exalted into trust;   55
His Counsel's oft convenient, seldom just.
Ev'n in the most sincere advice he gave
He had a grudging still to be a Knave.
The Frauds he learnt in his Fanatique years
Made him uneasy in his lawfull gears.   60
At best as little honest as he cou'd:
And, like white Witches, mischievously good.
To his first byass, longingly he leans;
And *rather* wou'd be great by wicked means.
Thus, fram'd for ill, he loos'd our Triple hold;   65
(Advice unsafe, precipitous, and bold.)
From hence those tears! that *Ilium* of our woe!
Who helps a pow'rfull Friend, fore-arms a Foe.
What wonder if the Waves prevail so far
When He cut down the Banks that made the bar?   70
Seas follow but their Nature to invade;
But He by Art our native Strength betray'd.
So *Sampson* to his Foe his force confest;
And, to be shorn, lay slumb'ring on her breast.
But, when this fatal Counsel, found too late,   75
Expos'd its Authour to the publique hate;
When his just Sovereign, by no impious way,
Cou'd be seduc'd to Arbitrary sway;
Forsaken of that hope, he shifts the sayle; ⎫
Drives down the Current with a pop'lar gale; ⎬   80
And shews the Fiend confess'd, without a vaile. ⎭
He preaches to the Crowd, that Pow'r is lent,
But not convey'd to Kingly Government;
That Claimes successive bear no binding force;
That Coronation Oaths are things of course;   85
Maintains the Multitude can never err;
And sets the People in the Papal Chair.
The reason's obvious; *Int'rest never lyes;* ⎫
The most have still their Int'rest in their eyes; ⎬
The pow'r is always theirs, and pow'r is ever wise. ⎭   90
Almighty Crowd, thou shorten'st all dispute;
Pow'r is thy Essence; Wit thy Attribute!
Nor Faith nor Reason make thee at a stay,
Thou leapst o'r all eternal truths, in thy *Pindarique* way!
Athens, no doubt, did righteously decide,   95
When *Phocion* and when *Socrates* were try'd:
As righteously they did those dooms repent;
Still they were wise, what ever way they went.
Crowds err not, though to both extremes they run;
To kill the Father, and recall the Son.   100
Some think the Fools were most, as times went then;

But now the World's o'r stock'd with prudent men.
The common Cry is ev'n Religion's Test;
The *Turk's* is, at *Constantinople*, best;
Idols in *India*, Popery at *Rome*;   105
And our own Worship onely true at home.
And true, but for the time, 'tis hard to know
How long we please it shall continue so.
This side to day, and that to morrow burns;
So all are God-a'mighties in their turns.   110
A Tempting Doctrine, plausible and new:
What Fools our Fathers were, if this be true!
Who, to destroy the seeds of Civil War,
Inherent right in Monarchs did declare:
And, that a lawfull Pow'r might never cease,   115
Secur'd Succession, to secure our Peace.
Thus, Property and Sovereign Sway, at last
In equal Balances were justly cast:
But this new *Jehu* spurs the hot mouth'd horse;
Instructs the Beast to know his native force;   120
To take the Bit between his teeth and fly
To the next headlong Steep of Anarchy.
Too happy *England*, if our good we knew;
Woud we possess the freedom we pursue!
The lavish Government can give no more: 125
Yet we repine; and plenty makes us poor.
God try'd us once; our Rebel-fathers fought;
He glutted 'em with all the pow'r they sought:
Till, mastered by their own usurping Brave,
The free-born Subject sunk into a Slave.   130
We loath our Manna, and we long for Quails;
Ah, what is man, when his own wish prevails!
How rash, how swift to plunge himself in ill;
Proud of his Pow'r, and boundless in his Will!
That Kings can doe no wrong we must believe: 135
None can they doe, and must they all receive?
Help Heaven! or sadly we shall see an hour,
When neither wrong nor right are in their pow'r!
Already they have lost their best defence,
The benefit of Laws, which they dispence.   140
No justice to their righteous Cause allow'd;
But baffled by an Arbitrary Crowd.
And Medalls grav'd, their Conquest to record,
The Stamp and Coyn of their adopted Lord.
    The Man who laugh'd but once, to see an Ass   145
Mumbling to make the cross-grain'd Thistles pass;
Might laugh again, to see a Jury chaw
The prickles of unpalatable Law.
The Witnesses, that, Leech-like, liv'd on bloud,

Sucking for them were med'cinally good;   150
But, when they fasten'd on *their* fester'd Sore, ⎫
Then, Justice and Religion they forswore;   ⎬
Their Mayden Oaths debauch'd into a Whore.   ⎭
Thus Men are rais'd by Factions, and decry'd;
And Rogue and Saint distinguish'd by their Side.   155
They rack ev'n Scripture to confess their Cause;
And plead a Call to preach, in spight of Laws.
But that's no news to the poor injur'd Page;
It has been us'd as ill in every Age:
And is constrain'd, with patience, all to take;   160
For what defence can Greek and Hebrew make?
Happy who can this talking Trumpet seize;
They make it speak whatever Sense they please!
'Twas fram'd, at first, our Oracle t' enquire;   ⎫
But, since our Sects in prophecy grow higher,   ⎬   165
The Text inspires not them; but they the Text inspire. ⎭
  London, thou great *Emporium* of our Isle,
O, thou too bounteous, thou too fruitfull *Nile*,
How shall I praise or curse to thy desert!
Or separate thy sound, from thy corrupted part!   170
I call'd thee *Nile*; the parallel will stand:
Thy tydes of Wealth o'rflow the fattend Land;
Yet Monsters from thy large increase we find;
Engender'd on the Slyme thou leav'st behind.
Sedition has not wholly seiz'd on thee;   175
Thy nobler Parts are from infection free.
Of *Israel*'s Tribes thou hast a numerous band;
But still the *Canaanite* is in the Land.
Thy military Chiefs are brave and true;
Nor are thy disinchanted Burghers few.   180
The Head is loyal which thy Heart commands;
But what's a Head with two such gouty Hands?
The wise and wealthy love the surest way;
And are content to thrive and to obey.
But Wisedom is to Sloath too great a Slave;   185
None are so busy as the Fool and Knave.
Those let me curse; what vengeance will they urge,
Whose Ordures neither Plague nor Fire can purge;
Nor sharp Experience can to duty bring,
Nor angry Heav'n, nor a forgiving King!   190
In Gospel phrase their Chapmen they betray:
Their Shops are Dens, the Buyer is their Prey.
The Knack of Trades is living on the Spoyl;
They boast, ev'n when each other they beguile.
Customes to steal is such a trivial thing,   195
That 'tis their Charter, to defraud their King.
All hands unite of every jarring Sect;

They cheat the Country first, and then infect.
They, for God's Cause their Monarchs dare dethrone;
And they'll be sure to make his Cause their own.   200
Whether the plotting Jesuite lay'd the plan
Of murth'ring Kings, or the *French* Puritan,
Our Sacrilegious Sects their Guides outgo;
And Kings and Kingly Pow'r wou'd murther too.
    What means their Trait'rous Combination less,   205
To plain t' evade, too shamefull to confess.
But Treason is not own'd when tis descry'd;
Successfull Crimes alone are justify'd.
The Men, who no Conspiracy wou'd find,
Who doubts, but had it taken, they had join'd.   210
Joyn'd, in a mutual Cov'nant of defence;
At first without, at last against their Prince.
If Sovereign Right by Sovereign Pow'r they scan,
The same bold Maxime holds in God and Man:
God were not safe, his Thunder cou'd they shun   215
He shou'd be forc'd to crown another Son.
Thus, when the Heir was from the Vineyard thrown;
The rich Possession was the Murth'rers own.
In vain to Sophistry they have recourse:
By proving theirs no Plot, they prove 'tis worse;   220
Unmask'd Rebellion, and audacious Force.
Which, though not Actual, yet all Eyes may see
'Tis working, in th' immediate Pow'r to be;
For, from pretended Grievances they rise,
First to dislike, and after to despise.   225
Then, *Cyclop*-like in humane Flesh to deal;
Chop up a Minister, at every meal:
Perhaps not wholly to melt down the King;
But clip his regal Rights within the Ring.
From thence, t' assume the pow'r of Peace and War;   230
And ease him by degrees of publique Care.
Yet, to consult his Dignity and Fame,
He shou'd have leave to exercise the Name;
And hold the Cards, while Commons play'd the game.
For what can Pow'r give more than Food and Drink,   235
To live at ease, and not be bound to think?
These are the cooler methods of their Crime;
But their hot Zealots think 'tis loss of time;
On utmost bounds of Loyalty they stand;
And grinn and whet like a *Croatian* Band;   240
That waits impatient for the last Command.
Thus Out-laws open Villany maintain:
They steal not, but in Squadrons scoure the Plain:
And, if their Pow'r the Passengers subdue;
The Most have right, the wrong is in the Few.   245

Such impious Axiomes foolishly they show;
For, in some Soyles Republiques will not grow:
Our Temp'rate Isle will no extremes sustain,
Of pop'lar Sway, or Arbitrary Reign:
But slides between them both into the best;   250
Secure in freedom, in a Monarch blest.
And though the Clymate, vex't with various Winds,
Works through our yielding Bodies, on our Minds,
The wholsome Tempest purges what it breeds;
To recommend the Calmness that succeeds.   255
    But thou, the Pander of the Peoples hearts,
(O Crooked Soul, and Serpentine in Arts,)
Whose blandishments a Loyal Land have whor'd,
And broke the Bonds she plighted to her Lord;
What Curses on thy blasted Name will fall!   260
Which Age to Age their Legacy shall call;
For all must curse the Woes that must descend on all.
Religion thou hast none: thy *Mercury*
Has pass'd through every Sect, or theirs through Thee.
But what thou giv'st, that Venom still remains;   265
And the pox'd Nation feels Thee in their Brains.
What else inspires the Tongues, and swells the Breasts
Of all thy bellowing Renegado Priests,
That preach up Thee for God; dispence thy Laws;
And with thy Stumm ferment their fainting Cause?   270
Fresh Fumes of Madness raise; and toile and sweat
To make the formidable Cripple great.
Yet, shou'd thy Crimes succeed, shou'd lawless Pow'r
Compass those Ends thy greedy Hopes devour,
Thy Canting Friends thy Mortal Foes wou'd be;   275
Thy God and Theirs will never long agree.
For thine, (if thou hast any,) must be one
That lets the World and Humane-kind alone:
A jolly God, that passes hours too well
To promise Heav'n, or threaten us with Hell.   280
That unconcern'd can at Rebellion sit;
And Wink at Crimes he did himself commit.
A Tyrant theirs; the Heav'n their Priesthood paints
A Conventicle of gloomy sullen Saints;
A Heav'n, like *Bedlam,* slovenly and sad;   285
Fore-doom'd for Souls, with false Religion, mad.
    Without a Vision Poets can fore-show
What all but Fools, by common Sense may know:
If true Succession from our Isle shou'd fail,
And Crowds profane, with impious Arms prevail,   290
Not Thou, nor those thy Factious Arts ingage
Shall reap that Harvest of Rebellious Rage,
With which thou flatter'st thy decrepit Age.

The swelling Poyson of the sev'ral Sects,
Which wanting vent, the Nations Health infects   295
Shall burst its Bag; and fighting out their way
The various Venoms on each other prey.
The *Presbyter*, puft up with spiritual Pride,
Shall on the Necks of the lewd Nobles ride:
His Brethren damn, the Civil Pow'r defy;   300
And parcel out Republique Prelacy.
But short shall be his Reign: his rigid Yoke
And Tyrant Pow'r will puny Sects provoke;
And Frogs and Toads, and all the Tadpole Train
Will croak to Heav'n for help, from this devouring Crane. 305
The Cut-throat Sword and clamorous Gown shall jar,
In shareing their ill-gotten Spoiles of War:
Chiefs shall be grudg'd the part which they pretend; ⎫
Lords envy Lords, and Friends with every Friend   ⎬
About their impious Merit shall contend.   ⎭   310
The surly Commons shall respect deny;
And justle Peerage out with Property.
Their Gen'ral either shall his Trust betray,
And force the Crowd to Arbitrary sway;
Or they suspecting his ambitious Aym,   ⎫   315
In hate of Kings shall cast anew the Frame;   ⎬
And thrust out *Collatine* that bore their Name.   ⎭
    Thus inborn Broyles the Factions wou'd ingage;
Or Wars of Exil'd Heirs, or Foreign Rage,   ⎫
Till halting Vengeance overtook our Age: ⎬   320
And our wild Labours, wearied into Rest,   ⎭
Reclin'd us on a rightfull Monarch's Breast.

Mac Flecknoe. Or a Satyr upon the True-Blew Protestant Poet, T. S.[1]

ALL humane things are subject to decay,
And, when Fate summons, Monarchs must obey:
This *Fleckno* found, who, like *Augustus*, young
Was call'd to Empire and had govern'd long:
In Prose and Verse was own'd, without dispute   5
Through all the realms of Non-sense, absolute.
This aged Prince now flourishing in Peace,
And blest with issue of a large increase,
Worn out with business, did at length debate
To settle the Succession of the State;   10

---

[1] Published in October, 1682. Text of second edition, 1684.

And pond'ring which of all his Sons was fit
To Reign, and wage immortal War with Wit,
Cry'd, 'tis resolv'd; for Nature pleads that He
Should onely rule, who most resembles me:
Sh——² alone my perfect image bears,   15
Mature in dullness from his tender years;
Sh—— alone of all my Sons is he
Who stands confirm'd in full stupidity.
The rest to some faint meaning make pretence,
But Sh—— never deviates into sense.   20
Some Beams of Wit on other souls may fall,
Strike through and make a lucid intervall;
But Sh——'s genuine night admits no ray,
His rising Fogs prevail upon the Day:
Besides, his goodly Fabrick fills the eye   25
And seems design'd for thoughtless Majesty:
Thoughtless as Monarch Oakes that shade the plain,
And, spread in solemn state, supinely reign.
Heywood and *Shirley* were but Types of thee,
Thou last great Prophet of Tautology: 30
Even I, a dunce of more renown than they,
Was sent before but to prepare thy way:
And coarsely clad in *Norwich* Drugget came
To teach the Nations in thy greater name.
My warbling Lute, the Lute I whilom strung,   35
When to King *John* of *Portugal* I sung,
Was but the prelude to that glorious day,
When thou on silver *Thames* did'st cut thy way,
With well tim'd oars before the Royal Barge,
Swelled with the Pride of thy Celestial charge;   40
And, big with Hymn, Commander of an Host,
The like was ne'er in *Epsom* blankets tost.
Methinks I see the new *Arion* Sail,
The Lute still trembling underneath thy nail.
At thy well sharpned thumb from Shore to Shore   45
The Treble squeaks for fear, the Bases roar:
Echoes from Pissing-Ally, Sh—— call,
And Sh—— they resound from *A[ston] Hall.*
About thy boat the little Fishes throng,
As at the Morning Toast that Floats along.   50
Sometimes, as Prince of thy Harmonious band,
Thou wield'st thy Papers in thy threshing hand.
St. *André*'s feet ne'er kept more equal time,
Not ev'n the feet of thy own *Psyche*'s rhime:
Though they in number as in sense excell,   55
So just, so like tautology they fell

---

² Thomas Shadwell.

That, pale with envy, *Singleton* forswore
The Lute and Sword which he in Triumph bore,
And vow'd he ne'er would act *Villerius* more.
Here stopt the good old Syre; and wept for joy,   60
In silent raptures of the hopefull boy.
All Arguments, but most his Plays, perswade
That for anointed dulness he was made.
    Close to the Walls which fair *Augusta* bind,
(The fair *Augusta* much to fears inclin'd)   65
An ancient fabrick raised t' inform the sight,
There stood of yore, and *Barbican* it hight:
A watch Tower once, but now, so Fate ordains,
Of all the Pile an empty name remains.
From its old Ruins Brothel-houses rise,   70
Scenes of lewd loves, and of polluted joys,
Where their vast Courts the Mother-Strumpets keep,
And, undisturbed by Watch, in silence sleep.
Near these a Nursery erects its head,
Where Queens are formed, and future Hero's bred;   75
Where unfledged Actors learn to laugh and cry,
Where infant Punks their tender voices try,
And little *Maximins* the Gods defy.
Great *Fletcher* never treads in Buskins here,
Nor greater Johnson dares in Socks appear.   80
But gentle *Simkin* just reception finds
Amidst this Monument of vanisht minds;
Pure Clinches, the suburbian Muse affords;
And *Panton* waging harmless war with words.
Here *Flecknoe*, as a place to Fame well known,   85
Ambitiously design'd his *Sh*——'s throne.
For ancient *Decker* prophesi'd long since,
That in this Pile should Reign a mighty Prince,
Born for a scourge of Wit, and flayle of Sense,
To whom true dulness should some *Psyches* owe,   90
But Worlds of *Misers* from his pen should flow;
Humorists and Hypocrites it should produce,
Whole *Raymond* Families and Tribes of *Bruce*.
    Now Empress Fame had publisht the renown
Of *Sh*——'s Coronation through the Town.   95
Rows'd by report of Fame, the Nations meet,
From near *Bun-Hill* and distant *Watling-street*.
No *Persian* Carpets spread th' imperial way,
But scatter'd Limbs of mangled Poets lay;
From dusty shops neglected Authors come,   100
Martyrs of Pies and Reliques of the Bum.
Much *Heywood, Shirley, Ogleby* there lay,
But loads of *Sh*—— almost choakt the way.
Bilk't *Stationers* for Yeomen stood prepar'd

And *H[erringman]* was Captain of the Guard.   105
The hoary Prince in Majesty appear'd,
High on a Throne of his own Labours rear'd.
At his right hand our young *Ascanius* sat
Rome's other hope and Pillar of the State.
His Brows thick fogs, instead of glories, grace,   110
And lambent dullness plaid around his face.
As *Hannibal* did to the Altars come,
Swore by his Syre a mortal Foe to *Rome*;
So *Sh——* swore, nor should his Vow bee vain,
That he till Death true dullness would maintain;   115
And, in his father's Right, and Realms defence,
Ne'er to have Peace with Wit, nor truce with Sense.
The King himself the sacred Unction made,
As King by Office, and as Priest by Trade:
In his sinister hand, instead of Ball,   120
He placed a mighty Mug of potent Ale;
Love's Kingdom to his right he did convey,
At once his Sceptre and his rule of Sway;
Whose righteous Lore the Prince had practis'd young
And from whose Loyns recorded *Psyche* sprung.   125
His temples, last, with Poppies were o'erspread,
That nodding seem'd to consecrate his head:
Just at that point of time, if Fame not lye,
On his left hand twelve reverend *Owls* did fly.
So *Romulus*, 'tis sung, by *Tyber*'s Brook,   130
Presage of Sway from twice six Vultures took.
Th' admiring throng loud acclamations make
And Omens of his future Empire take.
The Syre then shook the honours of his head,
And from his brows damps of oblivion shed   135
Full on the filial dullness: long he stood,
Repelling from his Breast the raging God;
At length burst out in this prophetick mood:
    Heavens bless my Son, from *Ireland* let him reign
To far *Barbadoes* on the Western main;   140
Of his Dominion may no end be known,
And greater than his Father's be his Throne.
Beyond loves Kingdom let him stretch his Pen;
He paused, and all the people cry'd *Amen.*
Then thus continued he, my son, advance   145
Still in new Impudence, new Ignorance.
Success let others teach, learn thou from me
Pangs without birth, and fruitless Industry.
Let *Virtuoso*'s in five years be Writ;
Yet not one thought accuse thy toyl of Wit.   150
Let gentle *George* in triumph tread the stage,
Make *Dorimant* betray, and *Loveit* rage;

Let *Cully, Cockwood, Fopling,* charm the Pit,
And in their folly show the Writers wit.
Yet still thy fools shall stand in thy defence   155
And justifie their Author's want of sense.
Let 'em be all by thy own model made
Of dulness and desire no foreign aid,
That they to future ages may be known,
Not Copies drawn, but Issue of thy own.   160
Nay let thy men of wit too be the same,
All full of thee, and differing but in name;
But let no alien *S-dl-y* interpose
To lard with wit thy hungry *Epsom* prose.
And when false flowers of *Rhetorick* thou would'st cull,   165
Trust Nature, do not labour to be dull;
But write thy best, and top; and in each line
Sir *Formal*'s oratory will be thine.
Sir *Formal*, though unsought, attends thy quill,
And does thy *Northern Dedications* fill.   170
Nor let false friends seduce thy mind to fame,
By arrogating *Johnson*'s Hostile name.
Let Father *Flecknoe* fire thy mind with praise
And Uncle *Ogleby* thy envy raise.
Thou art my blood, where *Johnson* has no part: 175
What share have we in Nature or in Art?
Where did his wit on learning fix a brand
And rail at Arts he did not understand?
Where made he love in Prince *Nicander*'s vein,
Or swept the dust in *Psyche*'s humble strain?   180
Where sold he Bargains, Whip-stitch, kiss my Arse,
Promis'd a Play and dwindled to a Farce?
When did his Muse from *Fletcher* scenes purloin,
As thou whole *Eth'ridg* dost transfuse to thine?
But so transfused as Oyls on waters flow,   185
His always floats above, thine sinks below.
This is thy Province, this thy wondrous way,
New Humours to invent for each new Play:
This is that boasted Byas of thy mind,
By which one way, to dullness, 'tis inclined,   190
Which makes thy writings lean on one side still,
And, in all changes, that way bends thy will.
Nor let thy mountain belly make pretence
Of likeness; thine's a tympany of sense.
A Tun of Man in thy large Bulk is writ,   195
But sure thou 'rt but a Kilderkin of wit.
Like mine thy gentle numbers feebly creep;
Thy Tragick Muse gives smiles, thy Comick sleep.
With whate'er gall thou settst thy self to write,
Thy inoffensive Satyrs never bite.   200

In thy fellonious heart though Venom lies,
It does but touch thy *Irish* pen, and dyes.
Thy Genius calls thee not to purchase fame
In keen Iambicks, but mild Anagram:
Leave writing Plays, and chuse for thy command   205
Some peacefull Province in Acrostick Land.
There thou maist wings display, and Altars raise,
And torture one poor word Ten thousand ways;
Or, if thou would'st thy diff'rent talents suit,
Set thy own Songs, and sing them to thy lute.   210
He said, but his last words were scarcely heard, ⎤
For *Bruce* and *Longvil* had a *Trap* prepar'd,   ⎬
And down they sent the yet declaiming Bard.   ⎦
Sinking he left his Drugget robe behind,
Borne upwards by a subterranean wind.   215
The Mantle fell to the young Prophet's part
With double portion of his Father's Art.

From The Second Part of Absalom and Achitophel.[1]

NEXT these, a Troop of buisy Spirits press,   310
Of little Fortunes and of Conscience Less;
With them the Tribe, whose Luxury had drain'd
Their Banks, in former Sequestrations gain'd:
Who Rich and Great by past Rebellions grew,
And long to fish the troubled Waves anew.   315
Some future Hopes, some present Payment draws,
To Sell their Conscience and espouse the Cause,
Such Stipends those vile Hirelings best befit,
Priests without Grace, and Poets without wit,
Shall that false *Hebronite* escape our Curse,   320
Judas[2] that keeps the Rebells Pension-Purse;
Judas that pays the Treason-writers Fee,
Judas that well deserves his Namesake's Tree;
Who at *Jerusalem's* own Gates Erects
His College for a Nursery of Sects.   325
Young Prophets with an early Care secures,
And with the Dung of his own Arts manures.
What have the Men of *Hebron*[3] here to doe?

---

[1] Published in November, 1682. Text of the first edition. The "Second Part" is mainly by Nahum Tate. Dryden is known to have contributed lines 310-509, which form part of a description of Achitophel's followers. See Preface.

[2] Robert Ferguson.

[3] Scotland.

What part in *Israels* promis'd Land have you?
Here *Phaleg*[4] the Lay *Hebronite* is come,   330
Cause like the rest he could not live at Home;
Who from his own Possessions cou'd not drain
An *Omer* even of *Hebronitish* Grain,
Here Struts it like a Patriot, and talks high
Of Injur'd Subjects, alter'd Property: 335
An Emblem of that buzzing Insect Just,
That mounts the Wheell, and thinks she raises Dust.
Can dry Bones Live? or *Skeletons* produce
The Vital Warmth of Cuckoldizing Juice?
Slim *Phaleg* cou'd, and at the Table fed,   340
Return'd the gratefull product to the Bed.
A Waiting-man to Trav'ling Nobles chose,
He, his own Laws wou'd Sawcily impose;
Till Bastinado'd back again he went,
To Learn those Manners he to Teach was sent.   345
Chastiz'd, he ought to have retreated Home,
But He reads politicks to *Absalom*.
For never *Hebronite*, though Kickt and Scorn'd,
To his own Country willingly return'd.
—But leaving famish'd *Phaleg* to be fed   350
And to talk Treason for his daily Bread,
Let *Hebron*, nay let Hell produce a Man
So made for Mischief as *Ben Jochanan*,[5]
A *Jew* of humble Parentage was He,
By Trade a Levite, though of low Degree: 355
His Pride no higher than the Desk aspir'd,
But for the Drudgery of Priests was hir'd
To Reade and Pray in Linen Ephod brave,
And pick up single Sheckles from the Grave.
Married at last, and finding Charge come faster,   360
He cou'd not live by God, but chang'd his Master:
Inspir'd by Want, was made a Factious Tool,
They Got a Villain, and we lost a Fool.
Still Violent, whatever Cause he took,
But most against the Party he forsook,   365
For Renegadoes, who ne'er turn by halves,
Are bound in Conscience to be double Knaves.
So this Prose-Prophet took most monstrous Pains
To let his Masters see he earn'd his Gains.
But as the Dev'l ows all his Imps a Shame,   370
He chose th' *Apostate* for his proper Theme;
With little Pains he made the Picture true,
And from Reflexion took the Rogue he drew.

---

[4] James Forbes.
[5] Samuel Johnson.

A wondrous Work, to prove the *Jewish* nation
In every Age a Murmuring Generation; 375
To trace 'em from their Infancy of Sinning,
And shew 'em Factious from their First Beginning;
To prove they cou'd Rebell, and Rail, and Mock,
Much to the Credit of the Chosen Flock;
A strong Authority which must Convince, 380
That Saints own no Allegiance to their Prince.
As 'tis a Leading-Card to make a Whore,
To prove her Mother had turn'd up before.
But tell me, did the Drunken Patriarch Bless
The Son that shew'd his Father's Nakedness? 385
Such Thanks the present Church thy Pen will give,
Which proves Rebellion was so Primitive.
Must Ancient Failings be Examples made,
Then Murtherers from *Cain* may learn their Trade.
As thou the Heathen and the Saint hast drawn, 390
Methinks th' Apostate was the better man:
And thy hot *Father* (waving my respect)
Not of a mother church but of a Sect.
And Such he needs must be of thy Inditing,
This Comes of drinking Asses milk and writing. 395
If *Balack*[6] should be cal'd to leave his place,
(As Profit is the loudest call of Grace,)
His Temple, dispossessed of one, would be
Replenish'd with seven Devils more by thee.
   Levi, thou art a load, I'll lay thee down, 400
And shew Rebellion bare, without a Gown;
Poor Slaves in metre, dull and adle-pated,
Who Rhime below ev'n *David's* Psalms translated.
Some in my Speedy pace I must outrun,
As lame *Mephibosheth*[7] the Wisard's Son; 405
To make quick way I'll Leap o'er heavy blocks,
Shun rotten *Uzza* as I woud the Pox;
And hasten *Og* and *Doeg* to rehearse,
Two Fools that Crutch their Feeble sense on Verse,
Who by my Muse, to all succeeding times 410
Shall live in spight of their own Dogrell Rhimes.
   Doeg,[8] though without knowing how or why,
Made still a blund'ring kind of Melody;
Spurd boldly on, and Dash'd through Thick and Thin,
Through Sense and Non-sense, never out nor in; 415
Free from all meaning, whether good or bad,
And in one word, Heroically mad:

---

[6] Gilbert Burnet.
[7] Samuel Pordage.
[8] Elkanah Settle.

He was too warm on Picking-work to dwell, ⎫
But Faggotted his Notions as they fell,   ⎬
And, if they Rhim'd and Rattl'd, all was well. ⎭   **420**
Spightfull he is not, though he wrote a Satyr,
For still there goes some *thinking* to ill-Nature:
He needs no more than Birds and Beasts to think,
All his occasions are to eat and drink.
If he call Rogue and Rascal from a Garrat,   **425**
He means you no more Mischief than a Parat:
The words for Friend and Foe alike were made,
To Fetter 'em in Verse is all his Trade.
For Almonds he'll cry Whore to his own Mother:
And call young *Absalom* King *David's* Brother.   **430**
Let him be Gallows-Free by my consent,
And nothing suffer, since he nothing meant:
Hanging Supposes humane Soul and reason,
This Animal's below committing Treason:
Shall he be hang'd who never cou'd Rebell?   **435**
That's a preferment for *Achitophel.*
The Woman that Committed Buggary,
Was rightly Sentenc'd by the Law to die;
But 'twas hard Fate that to the Gallows led
The Dog that never heard the Statute read.   **440**
Railing in other Men may be a crime,
But ought to pass for mere instinct in him;
Instinct he follows and no farther knows,
For to write Verse with him is to *Transprose.*
'Twere pity treason at his Door to lay   **445**
Who *makes Heaven's gate a Lock to its own Key:*
Let him rayl on, let his invective muse
Have four and Twenty letters to abuse,
Which if he Jumbles to one line of Sense,
Indict him of a Capital Offence.   **450**
In Fire-works give him leave to vent his spight,
Those are the only Serpents he can write;
The height of his ambition is we know
But to be Master of a Puppet-show;
On that one Stage his works may yet appear,   **455**
And a months Harvest keeps him all the Year.
   Now stop your noses, Readers, all and some, ⎫
For here's a tun of Midnight work to come,   ⎬
Og[9] from a Treason Tavern rowling home. ⎭
Round as a Globe, and Liquored ev'ry chink,   **460**
Goodly and Great he Sayls behind his Link;
With all this Bulk there's nothing lost in *Og,*

---

[9] Thomas Shadwell.

For ev'ry inch that is not Fool is Rogue:
A Monstrous mass of foul corrupted matter,
As all the Devils had spew'd to make the batter. 465
When wine has given him courage to Blaspheme,
He curses God, but God before Curst him;
And if man cou'd have reason, none has more,
That made his Paunch so rich and him so poor.
With wealth he was not trusted, for Heav'n knew 470
What 'twas of Old to pamper up a *Jew*;
To what would he on Quail and Pheasant swell,
That ev'n on Tripe and Carrion cou'd rebell?
But though Heaven made him poor, (with rev'rence speaking,)
He never was a Poet of God's making; 475
The Midwife laid her hand on his Thick Skull,
With this Prophetick blessing—*Be thou Dull;*
Drink, Swear, and Roar, forbear no lew'd delight
Fit for thy Bulk, doe anything but write.
Thou art of lasting Make, like thoughtless men, 480
A strong Nativity—but for the Pen;
Eat Opium, mingle Arsenick in thy Drink,
Still thou mayst live, avoiding Pen and Ink.
I see, I see, 'tis Counsell given in vain,
For Treason botcht in Rhime will be thy bane; 485
Rhime is the Rock on which thou art to wreck,
'Tis fatal to thy Fame and to thy Neck.
Why should thy Metre good King *David* blast?
A Psalm of his will Surely be thy last.
Dar'st thou presume in verse to meet thy foes, 490
Thou whom the Penny Pamphlet foil'd in prose?
Doeg, whom God for Mankinds mirth has made,
O'er-tops thy tallent in thy very Trade;
Doeg to thee, thy paintings are so Course,
A Poet is, though he's the Poets Horse. 495
A Double Noose thou on thy Neck dost pull
For writing Treason and for Writing dull;
To die for Faction is a common Evil,
But to be hang'd for Non-sense is the Devil.
Hadst thou the Glories of thy King exprest, 500
Thy praises had been Satyr at the best;
But thou in Clumsy verse, unlickt, unpointed,
Hast Shamefully defi'd the Lord's Anointed:
I will not rake the Dunghill of thy Crimes,
For who would reade thy Life that reads thy rhimes? 505
But of King *David*'s Foes be this the Doom,
May all be like the Young-man *Absalom*;
And for my Foes may this their Blessing be,
To talk like *Doeg* and to Write like Thee.

Religio Laici; or, A Layman's Faith. A Poem[1]

DIM, as the borrow'd beams of Moon and Stars
To *lonely, weary, wandring* Travellers,
Is *Reason* to the *Soul:* And as on high,
Those rowling Fires *discover* but the Sky
Not light us *here*; so *Reason's* glimmering Ray ⎤   5
Was lent, not to *assure* our *doubtfull* way,   ⎬
But *guide* us upward to a *better Day.*   ⎦
And as those nightly Tapers disappear
When Day's bright Lord ascends our Hemisphere;
So pale grows *Reason* at *Religions* sight;   10
So *dyes*, and so *dissolves* in *Supernatural Light.*
Some few, whose Lamp shone brighter, have been led
From Cause to Cause, to *Natures* secret head;
And found that *one first principle* must be:
But *what*, or *who*, that *UNIVERSAL HE*;   15
Whether some *Soul* incompassing this Ball
Unmade, unmov'd; yet *making, moving All*;
Or various *Atom's*, interfering Dance
Leapt into *Form*, (the Noble work of *Chance*;)
Or this great *All* was from *Eternity*;   ⎤   20
Not ev'n the *Stagirite* himself could see;   ⎬
And *Epicurus Guess'd* as well as He: ⎦
As *blindly grop'd* they for a *future State*;
As *rashly Judg'd* of *Providence* and *Fate:*
But least of all could their Endeavours find   25
What most concern'd the good of Humane kind:
For *Happiness* was never to be found;
But vanish'd from 'em, like Enchanted ground.
One thought *Content* the Good to be enjoy'd:
This, every little *Accident* destroy'd: 30
The *wiser Madmen* did for *Vertue* toyl:
A Thorny, or at best a barren Soil:
In *Pleasure* some their glutton Souls would steep; ⎤
But found their Line too short, the Well too deep; ⎬
And leaky Vessels which no *Bliss* cou'd keep.   ⎦   35
Thus, *anxious Thoughts* in *endless Circles* roul,
Without a *Centre* where to fix the *Soul:*
In this wilde Maze their vain Endeavours end.
How can the *less* the *Greater* comprehend?
Or *finite Reason* reach *Infinity?*   40
For what cou'd *Fathom GOD* were *more* than *He.*
   The *Deist* thinks he stands on firmer ground;
Cries ευρεκα: the mighty Secret's found:

---

[1] Published in November, 1682. Text of first edition.

God is that *Spring* of *Good*; *Supreme*, and *Best*;
We, made to *serve*, and in that Service *blest*;   **45**
If so, some *Rules* of Worship must be given,
Distributed alike to all by Heaven:
Else *God* were *partial*, and to *some* deny'd
The Means his Justice shou'd for *all* provide.
This *general Worship* is to *PRAISE*, and *PRAY*:   **50**
One part to *borrow* Blessings, one to *pay*:
And when frail Nature slides into *Offence*,
The *Sacrifice* for *Crimes* is *Penitence*.
Yet, since th' Effects of Providence, we find
Are variously dispens'd to Humane kind;   **55**
That *Vice Triumphs*, and *Vertue suffers* here,
(A Brand that Sovereign Justice cannot bear;)
Our Reason prompts us to a *future* State:
The *last Appeal* from *Fortune*, and from *Fate*:
Where God's all-righteous ways will be declar'd;   **60**
The *Bad* meet *Punishment*, the *Good*, *Reward*.
    Thus Man by his own strength to Heaven wou'd soar:
And wou'd not be Oblig'd to God for more.
Vain, wretched Creature, how art thou misled
To think thy Wit these God-like Notions bred!   **65**
These Truths are not the product of thy Mind,
But dropt from Heaven, and of a Nobler kind.
Reveal'd Religion first inform'd thy Sight,
And *Reason* saw not, till *Faith* sprung the Light.
Hence all thy *Natural Worship* takes the *Source*:   **70**
'Tis *Revelation* what thou thinkst *Discourse*.
Else, how com'st *Thou* to see these truths so clear,
Which so obscure to *Heathens* did appear?
Not *Plato* these, nor *Aristotle* found:
Nor He whose Wisedom *Oracles* renown'd.   **75**
Hast thou a Wit so deep, or so sublime,
Or canst thou lower dive, or higher climb?
Canst *Thou*, by *Reason*, more of *God-head* know
Than *Plutarch*, *Seneca*, or *Cicero?*
Those Gyant Wits, in happyer Ages born,   **80**
(When *Arms*, and *Arts* did *Greece* and *Rome* adorn)
Knew no such *Systeme*: no such Piles cou'd raise
Of *Natural Worship*, built on *Pray'r* and *Praise*,
To One sole GOD.
Nor did Remorse, to Expiate Sin, prescribe: **85**
But slew their fellow Creatures for a Bribe:
The guiltless *Victim* groan'd for their Offence;
And *Cruelty*, and *Blood* was *Penitence*.
If *Sheep* and *Oxen* cou'd Attone for Men
Ah! at how cheap a rate the *Rich* might Sin!   **90**
And great Oppressours might Heavens Wrath beguile

By offering his own Creatures for a Spoil!
  Dar'st thou, poor Worm, offend *Infinity?*
And must the Terms of Peace be given by *Thee?*
Then *Thou* art *Justice* in the *last Appeal*;   95
Thy easie God instructs Thee to *rebell:*
And, like a King remote, and weak, must take
What Satisfaction *Thou* art pleas'd to make.
  But if there be a *Pow'r* too *Just*, and *strong*
To wink at *Crimes*, and bear unpunish'd *Wrong*;   100
Look humbly upward, see his Will disclose
The *Forfeit* first, and then the *Fine* impose:
A *Mulct thy* Poverty cou'd never pay
Had not *Eternal Wisedom* found the way:
And with Cœlestial Wealth supply'd thy Store: 105
His Justice makes the *Fine, his Mercy* quits the *Score.*
See God descending in thy Humane Frame;
Th' *offended*, suff'ring in th' *Offenders* Name:
All thy Misdeeds to him imputed see,
And all his Righteousness devolv'd on thee.   110
  For granting we have Sin'd, and that th' offence
Of *Man*, is made against *Omnipotence*,
Some Price, that bears *proportion*, must be paid;
And *Infinite* with *Infinite* be weigh'd.
See then the *Deist lost: Remorse* for *Vice*,   115
Not paid, or *paid, inadequate* in price:
What farther means can *Reason* now direct,
Or what Relief from *humane Wit* expect?
That shews us *sick*; and sadly are we sure
Still to be *Sick*, till *Heav'n* reveal the *Cure:*   120
If then *Heaven's Will* must needs be understood,
(Which must, if we want *Cure*, and *Heaven*, be *Good*)
Let all Records of *Will reveal'd* be shown; ⎫
With *Scripture*, all in equal ballance thrown, ⎬
And *our one Sacred Book* will be *That one.* ⎭   125
  Proof needs not here, for whether we compare
That Impious, Idle, Superstitious Ware
Of *Rites, Lustrations, Offerings*, (which before,
In various Ages, various Countries bore)
With *Christian Faith* and *Vertues*, we shall find   130
None answ'ring the great ends of humane kind
But *This one Rule of Life: That* shews us best
How *God* may be *appeas'd*, and *Mortals blest.*
Whether from length of *Time* its worth we draw,
The *World* is scarce more *Ancient* than the *Law:*   135
Heav'ns early Care prescrib'd for every Age;
First, in the *Soul*, and after, in the *Page.*
Or, whether more abstractedly we look,
Or on the *Writers*, or the *written Book*,

Whence, but from *Heav'n*, cou'd men unskill'd in Arts,   140
In several Ages born, in several parts,
Weave such *agreeing Truths?* or *how*, or *why*
Shou'd *all* conspire to cheat us with a *Lye?*
Unask'd their *Pains, ungratefull* their *Advice*,
Starving their *Gain*, and *Martyrdom* their *Price*.   145
   If on the Book it self we cast our view,
Concurrent Heathens prove the Story *True:*
The *Doctrine, Miracles;* which must convince,
For *Heav'n* in *Them* appeals to *humane Sense:*
And though they *prove* not, they *Confirm* the Cause,   150
When what is *Taught* agrees with *Natures Laws.*
   Then for the *Style; Majestick* and *Divine*,
It speaks no less than God in every Line:
Commanding words; whose *Force* is still the same
As the first *Fiat* that produc'd our Frame.   155
All Faiths *beside*, or did by *Arms* ascend;
Or *Sense* indulg'd has made *Mankind* their *Friend:*
This *onely* Doctrine does our *Lusts* oppose:
Unfed by Natures Soil, in which it grows;
Cross to our *Interests*, curbing Sense, and Sin;   160
Oppress'd without, and undermin'd within,
It thrives through pain; its own Tormentours tires;
And with a stubborn patience still aspires.
To what can *Reason* such Effects assign
Transcending *Nature,* but to *Laws Divine?*   165
Which in that Sacred Volume are contain'd;
Sufficient, clear, and for that use ordain'd.
   But stay: the *Deist* here will urge anew,
No *Supernatural Worship* can be *True:*
Because a *general Law* is that alone   170
Which must to *all*, and every *where* be known:
A Style so large as not *this* Book can claim
Nor ought that bears *reveal'd* Religions *Name.*
'Tis said the sound of a *Messiah's Birth*
Is gone through all the habitable Earth: 175
But still that Text must be confin'd alone
To what was *Then* inhabited, and known:
And what Provision cou'd from *thence* accrue
To *Indian* Souls, and Worlds discover'd *New?*
In other parts it helps, that Ages past,   180
The Scriptures there were *known*, and were *imbrac'd*,
Till Sin spread once again the Shades of Night:
What's that to these who never *saw* the Light?
   Of all Objections this indeed is chief
To startle Reason, stagger frail Belief: 185
We grant, 'tis true, that Heav'n from humane Sense
Has hid the secret paths of *Providence:*

But *boundless Wisdom, boundless Mercy,* may
Find ev'n for those *be-wildred* Souls, a *way:*
If from his *Nature Foes* may Pity claim,   190
Much more may *Strangers* who ne'er heard his *Name.*
And though *no Name* be for *Salvation* known,
But that of his *Eternal Sons* alone;
Who knows how far transcending Goodness can
Extend the *Merits* of *that Son* to *Man?*   195
Who knows what *Reasons* may his *Mercy* lead;
Or *Ignorance invincible* may plead?
Not onely *Charity* bids hope the *best,*
But *more* the great Apostle has exprest:
That, if the Gentiles, (whom no Law inspir'd,)   200
By Nature did what was by *Law requir'd;*
They, who the written Rule had never known,
Were to themselves both Rule and Law alone:
To Natures plain indictment they shall plead;
And, by their Conscience, be condemn'd or freed.   205
Most righteous Doom! because a *Rule reveal'd*
Is *none* to *Those,* from whom it was *conceal'd.*
Then those who follow'd *Reasons* Dictates right;
Liv'd up, and lifted high their *Natural Light;*
With *Socrates* may see their Maker's Face,   210
While Thousand *Rubrick-Martyrs* want a place.
    Nor does it baulk my *Charity,* to find
Th' *Egyptian* Bishop of another mind:
For, though his *Creed Eternal Truth* contains,
'Tis hard for *Man* to doom to *endless pains*   215
All who believ'd not all, his Zeal requir'd;
Unless he first cou'd prove he was inspir'd.
Then let us either think he meant to say
This Faith, where *publish'd,* was the onely way;
Or else conclude that, *Arius* to confute,   220
The good old Man, too eager in dispute,
Flew high; and as his *Christian* Fury rose
Damn'd all for *Hereticks* who durst *oppose.*

    Thus far my Charity this path has try'd;
(A much unskilfull, but well meaning guide:)   225
Yet what they are, ev'n these crude thoughts were bred
By reading that, which better thou hast read.
Thy Matchless Author's work: which thou, my Friend,[2]
By well translating better dost commend:
Those youthfull hours which, of thy Equals most   230
In *Toys* have *squander'd,* or in *Vice* have *lost,*
Those hours hast thou to Nobler use employ'd;

---

[2] Richard Simon's *Critical History of the Old Testament,* recently translated from
the French by Henry Dickinson, to whom Dryden addressed his poem.

And the severe Delights of Truth enjoy'd.
Witness this weighty Book, in which appears
The crabbed Toil of many thoughtfull years,   235
Spent by thy Authour, in the Sifting Care
Of *Rabbins* old Sophisticated Ware
From Gold Divine; which he who well can sort
May afterwards make *Algebra* a Sport.
A Treasure, which if *Country-Curates* buy,   240
They *Junius*, and *Tremellius* may defy:
Save pains in various readings, and Translations;
And without *Hebrew* make most learn'd quotations.
A Work so full with various Learning fraught,
So nicely pondred, yet so strongly wrought,   245
As Natures height and Arts last hand requir'd:
As much as Man cou'd compass, uninspir'd.
Where we may see what *Errours* have been made
Both in the *Copiers* and *Translaters Trade:*
How *Jewish*, *Popish*, Interests have prevail'd,   250
And where *Infallibility* has *fail'd*.
    For some, who have his secret meaning ghes'd,
Have found our Authour not too *much a Priest:*
For *Fashion-sake* he seems to have recourse
To *Pope*, and *Councils*, and *Traditions* force: 255
But he that *old* Traditions cou'd subdue,
Cou'd not but find the weakness of the *New:*
If *Scripture*, though deriv'd from *heav'nly birth*,
Has been but carelesly preserv'd on *Earth*;
If *God's own People*, who of *God* before   260
Knew what we know, and had been promis'd more,
In fuller Terms, of Heaven's assisting Care,
And who did neither *Time*, nor *Study* spare
To keep this Book *untainted, unperplext*;
Let in gross *Errours* to corrupt the *Text:*   265
Omitted *paragraphs*, embroyl'd the *Sense*;
With vain *Traditions* stopt the gaping Fence,
Which every common hand pull'd up with ease:
What Safety from such *brushwood-helps* as these?
If *written words* from time are not secur'd,   270
How can we think have *oral Sounds* endur'd?
Which *thus* transmitted, if *one* Mouth has fail'd,
Immortal Lyes on *Ages* are intail'd:
And that some such have been, is prov'd too plain;
If we consider *Interest, Church*, and *Gain*.   275
    Oh but says one, *Tradition* set aside,
Where can we hope for an *unerring Guid?*
For since th' *original* Scripture has been lost,
All Copies *disagreeing, maim'd* the *most*,

Or *Christian Faith* can have no *certain* ground,   280
Or *Truth* in *Church Tradition* must be found.
  Such an *Omniscient* Church we wish indeed;
'Twere worth *Both Testaments*, and cast in the *Creed*:
But if *this Mother* be a *Guid* so sure,
As can all *doubts resolve*, all *truth secure*,   285
Then her *Infallibility*, as well
Where Copies are *corrupt*, or *lame*, can tell;
Restore *lost Canon* with as little pains,
As *truly explicate* what still *remains*:
Which yet no *Council* dare *pretend* to doe; ⎫   290
Unless like *Esdras*, they cou'd *write* it new: ⎬
Strange Confidence, still to *interpret* true, ⎭
Yet not be sure that all they have explain'd,
Is in the blest *Original* contain'd.
More Safe, and much more modest 'tis, to say   295
God wou'd not leave Mankind without a way:
And that the *Scriptures*, though not *every where*
Free from Corruption, or intire, or clear,
Are uncorrupt, sufficient, clear, intire,
In *all* things which our needfull *Faith* require.   300
If *others* in the *same Glass better* see
'Tis for *Themselves* they look, but not for *me:*
For *MY* Salvation must its Doom receive
Not from what *OTHERS*, but what *I* believe.
  Must *all Tradition* then be set aside?   305
This to affirm were Ignorance, or Pride.
Are there not many points, some needfull sure
To saving Faith, that Scripture leaves obscure?
Which every Sect will wrest a several way
(For what *one* Sect Interprets, *all* Sects *may:*)   310
We hold, and say we prove from Scripture plain, ⎫
That *Christ* is *GOD*; the bold *Socinian* ⎬
From the *same* Scripture urges he's but *MAN*. ⎭
Now what Appeal can end th' important Suit;
Both parts *talk* loudly, but the *Rule* is *mute?*   315
  Shall I speak plain, and in a Nation free
Assume an honest *Layman's Liberty?*
I think (according to my little Skill,
To my own Mother-Church submitting still)
That many have been sav'd, and many may,   320
Who never heard this Question brought in play.
Th' *unletter'd* Christian, who believes in *gross*,
Plods on to *Heaven*; and ne'er is at a loss:
For the *Streight-gate* wou'd be made *streighter* yet,
Were *none* admitted there but men of *Wit*.   325
The few, by Nature form'd, with Learning fraught,
Born to instruct, as others to be taught,

Must Study well the Sacred Page; and see
Which Doctrine, this, or that, does best agree
With the whole Tenour of the Work Divine: 330
And plainlyest points to Heaven's reveal'd Design:
Which Exposition flows from *genuine Sense*;
And which is *forc'd* by *Wit* and *Eloquence*.
Not that Traditions parts are useless here:
When general, old, disinteress'd and clear: 335
That Ancient Fathers thus expound the Page,
Gives *Truth* the reverend Majesty of *Age:*
Confirms its force, by biding every *Test;*
For best *Authority's* next *Rules* are *best.*
And still the nearer to the Spring we go   340
More limpid, more unsoyl'd the Waters flow.
Thus, *first Traditions* were a proof alone;
Cou'd we be *certain* such they *were*, so *known:*
But since some Flaws in long descent may be,
They make not *Truth* but *Probability.*   345
Even *Arius* and *Pelagius* durst provoke
To what the *Centuries preceding* spoke.
Such difference is there in an oft-told Tale:
But Truth by its own Sinews will prevail.
Tradition written therefore more commends   350
Authority, than what from *Voice* descends:
And this, as perfect as its kind can be,
Rouls down to us the Sacred History:
Which, from the *Universal Church receiv'd*,
Is *try'd*, and *after*, for its *self* believ'd.   355
    The partial *Papists* wou'd infer from hence
Their Church, in last resort, shou'd Judge the *Sense.*
But first they wou'd assume, with wondrous Art,
Themselves to be the *whole*, who are but *part*
Of that vast Frame, the Church; yet grant they were   360
The handers down, can they from thence infer
A right t' interpret? or wou'd they alone
Who brought the Present, claim it for their own?
The *Book's* a *Common Largess* to *Mankind*;
Not more for *them*, than *every* Man design'd: 365
The *welcome News* is in the *Letter* found;
The *Carrier's* not Commission'd to *expound.*
It *speaks* it *Self*, and what it does contain,
In all things *needfull* to be *known*, is *plain.*
    In times o'ergrown with Rust and Ignorance,   370
A gainfull Trade their Clergy did advance:
When want of Learning kept the *Laymen* low,
And none but *Priests* were *Authoriz'd* to *know:*
When what small Knowledge was, in them did dwell;
And he a *God* who cou'd but *Reade* or *Spell*;   375

Then *Mother Church* did mightily prevail:
She parcel'd out the Bible by *retail:*
But still *expounded* what She *sold* or *gave;*
To keep it in *her Power* to *Damn* and *Save:*
Scripture was *scarce,* and as the Market went,   380
Poor *Laymen* took *Salvation* on *Content;*
As needy men take Money, good or bad:
God's Word they had not, but the *Priests* they had.
Yet, whate'er *false Conveyances* they made,
The *Lawyer* still was *certain* to be paid.   385
In those dark times they learn'd their knack so well,
That by long use they grew *Infallible:*
At last, a knowing Age began t' enquire
If *they* the *Book,* or *That* did *them* inspire:
And, making narrower search they found, thô late,   390
That what they thought the *Priest*'s was *Their* Estate:
Taught by the *Will produc'd,* (the written Word)
How long they had been *cheated* on *Record.*
Then, every man who saw the Title fair,
Claim'd a Child's part, and put in for a Share: 395
Consulted Soberly his private good;
And sav'd himself as cheap as e'er he cou'd.
    'Tis true, my Friend, (and far be Flattery hence)
This good had full as bad a Consequence:
The Book thus put in every vulgar hand,   400
Which each presum'd he best cou'd understand,
The *Common Rule* was made the *common Prey;*
And at the mercy of the *Rabble* lay.
The tender Page with horney Fists was gaul'd;
And he was gifted most that loudest baul'd: 405
The *Spirit* gave the *Doctoral Degree:* ⎫
And every member of a *Company*   ⎬
Was of *his Trade,* and of the *Bible free.* ⎭
Plain *Truths* enough for needfull *use* they found;
But men wou'd still be itching to *expound:*   410
Each was ambitious of th' obscurest place,
No measure ta'n from *Knowledge,* all from *GRACE.*
Study and *Pains* were now no more their Care;
Texts were explain'd by *Fasting,* and by *Prayer:*
This was the Fruit the *private Spirit* brought;   415
Occasion'd by *great Zeal,* and *little Thought.*
While Crouds unlearn'd, with rude Devotion warm,
About the Sacred Viands buz and swarm.
The *Fly-blown Text* creates a *crawling Brood;*
And turns to *Maggots* what was meant for *Food.*   420
A Thousand daily Sects rise up, and dye;
A Thousand more the perish'd Race supply:
So all we make of Heavens discover'd Will

Is, not to have it, or to use it ill.
The Danger's much the same; on several Shelves   425
If *others* wreck *us*, or *we* wreck our *selves*.
　What then remains, but, waving each Extreme,
The Tides of Ignorance, and Pride to stem?
Neither so rich a Treasure to forgo;
Nor proudly seek beyond our pow'r to know: 430
Faith is not built on disquisitions vain;
The things we *must* believe, are *few*, and *plain:*
But since men *will* believe more than they *need*;
And every man will make *himself* a Creed:
In doubtfull questions 'tis the safest way   435
To learn what unsuspected Ancients say:
For 'tis not likely *we* shou'd higher Soar
In search of Heav'n, than *all the Church before:*
Nor can we be deceiv'd, unless we see
The *Scripture*, and the *Fathers disagree.*   440
If after all, they stand suspected still,
(For no man's Faith depends upon his Will;)
'Tis some Relief, that points not clearly known,
Without much hazard may be let alone:
And, after hearing what our Church can say,   445
If still our Reason runs another way,
That private Reason 'tis more Just to curb,
Than by Disputes the publick Peace disturb.
For points obscure are of small use to learn:
But *Common quiet* is *Mankind's concern.*   450
　Thus have I made my own Opinions clear:
Yet neither Praise expect, nor Censure fear:
And this unpolish'd, rugged Verse, I chose;
As fittest for Discourse, and nearest Prose:
For, while from *Sacred Truth* I do not swerve,   455
Tom Sternhold's, or *Tom Sha—ll's Rhimes* will serve.

Epilogue Spoken at Oxford by Mrs. Marshall[1]

OFT has our Poet wisht, this happy Seat
Might prove his fading Muses last retreat.
I wonder'd at his wish, but now I find
He sought for quiet, and content of mind;
Which noiseful Towns, and Courts can never know,   5
And only in the shades like Laurels grow.
Youth, e'er it sees the World, here studies rest,

---

[1] Published in *Miscellanies,* 1684. Text of Tonson's edition of Dryden's *Poems,* 1701.

And Age returning thence concludes it best.
What wonder if we court that happiness
Yearly to share, which hourly you possess,   10
Teaching ev'n you, (while the vext World we show,)
Your Peace to value more, and better know?
'Tis all we can return for favours past,
Whose holy Memory shall ever last,
For Patronage from him whose care presides   15
O'er every noble Art, and every Science guides:
Bathurst, a name the learn'd with reverence know,
And scarcely more to his own *Virgil* owe.
Whose Age enjoys but what his Youth deserv'd,
To rule those Muses whom before he serv'd: 20
His Learning, and untainted Manners too
We find (*Athenians*) are deriv'd to you;
Such ancient hospitality there rests,
In yours, as dwelt in the first *Grecian* Breasts,
Whose kindness was Religion to their Guests.   25
Such Modesty did to our Sex appear,
As had there been no Laws we need not fear,
Since each of you was our Protector here.
Converse so chast, and so strict Virtue shown,
As might *Apollo* with the Muses own.   30
Till our return we must despair to find
Judges so just, so knowing, and so kind.

To the Memory of Mr. Oldham[1]

FAREWEL, too little and too lately known,
Whom I began to think and call my own;
For sure our Souls were near ally'd, and thine
Cast in the same Poetick mould as mine.
One common Note on either Lyre did strike,   5
And Knaves and Fools we both abhorr'd alike:
To the same Goal did both our Studies drive,
The last set out the soonest did arrive.
Thus *Nisus* fell upon the slippery place,
Whilst his young Friend perform'd and won the Race.   10
O early ripe! to thy abundant store
What could advancing Age have added more?
It might (what Nature never gives the young)
Have taught the numbers of thy native Tongue.
But Satyr needs not those, and Wit will shine   15
Through the harsh cadence of a rugged line.

[1] Published in *The Remains of Mr. John Oldham*, 1684. Text of first edition.

A noble Error, and but seldom made,
When Poets are by too much force betray'd.
Thy generous fruits, though gather'd ere their prime,
Still shew'd a quickness; and maturing time   20
But mellows what we write to the dull sweets of Rime.
Once more, hail, and farewel; farewel, thou young,
But ah too short, *Marcellus* of our Tongue;
Thy Brows with Ivy, and with Laurels bound;
But Fate and gloomy Night encompass thee around.   25

Horat. Ode 29. Book 3. Paraphras'd in *Pindarique* Verse[1]

DESCENDED of an ancient Line,
   That long the *Tuscan* Scepter sway'd,
Make haste to meet the generous wine,
   Whose piercing is for thee delay'd:
The rosie wreath is ready made;   5
   And artful hands prepare
The fragrant *Syrian* Oyl, that shall perfume thy hair.

When the Wine sparkles from a far,
   And the well-natur'd Friend cries, come away;
Make haste, and leave thy business and thy care,   10
   No mortal int'rest can be worth thy stay.

Leave for a while thy costly Country Seat;
   And, to be Great indeed, forget
The nauseous pleasures of the Great:
   Make haste and come: 15
Come, and forsake thy cloying store;
   Thy Turret that surveys, from high,
The smoke, and wealth, and noise of *Rome*;
   And all the busie pageantry
That wise men scorn, and fools adore: 20
Come, give thy Soul a loose, and taste the pleasures of the poor.

Sometimes 'tis grateful to the Rich, to try
A short vicissitude, and fit of Poverty:
   A savoury Dish, a homely Treat,
   Where all is plain, where all is neat,   25
   Without the stately spacious Room,
The *Persian* Carpet, or the *Tyrian* Loom,
Clear up the cloudy foreheads of the Great.

---

[1] Published in *Sylvae*, 1685. Text of first edition.

The Sun is in the Lion mounted high;
 The *Syrian* Star   30
  Barks from afar;
 And with his sultry breath infects the Sky;
The ground below is parch'd, the heav'ns above us fry.
 The Shepheard drives his fainting Flock,
 Beneath the covert of a Rock;   35
 And seeks refreshing Rivulets nigh:
 The *Sylvans* to their shades retire,
Those very shades and streams new shades and streams require;
And want a cooling breeze of wind to fan the raging fire.

 Thou, what befits the new Lord May'r,   40
 And what the City Faction dare,
 And what the *Gallique* Arms will do,
 And what the Quiver bearing Foe,
 Art anxiously inquisitive to know:
But God has, wisely, hid from humane sight   45
 The dark decrees of future fate;
 And sown their seeds in depth of night;
He laughs at all the giddy turns of State;
When Mortals search too soon, and fear too late.

 Enjoy the present smiling hour;   50
 And put it out of Fortunes pow'r:
 The tide of bus'ness, like the running stream,
 Is sometimes high, and sometimes low,
 A quiet ebb, or a tempestuous flow,
  And alwayes in extream.   55
 Now with a noiseless gentle course
 It keeps within the middle Bed;
 Anon it lifts aloft the head,
And bears down all before it, with impetuous force:
 And trunks of Trees come rowling down, 60
 Sheep and their Folds together drown:
 Both House and Homested into Seas are borne,
 And Rocks are from their old foundations torn,
And woods made thin with winds, their scatter'd honours mourn.

 Happy the Man, and happy he alone,   65
 He, who can call to day his own:
 He, who, secure within, can say,
 Tomorrow do thy worst, for I have liv'd today.
 Be fair, or foul, or rain, or shine,
 The joys I have possest, in spight of fate, are mine. 70
 Not Heav'n it self upon the past has pow'r;
But what has been, has been, and I have had my hour.

Fortune, that with malicious joy,
  Does Man her slave oppress,
Proud of her Office to destroy,   75
  Is seldome pleas'd to bless.
Still various, and unconstant still;
But with an inclination to be ill;
  Promotes, degrades, delights in strife,
  And makes a Lottery of life.   80
I can enjoy her while she's kind;
But when she dances in the wind,
  And shakes her wings, and will not stay,
  I puff the Prostitute away:
The little or the much she gave, is quietly resign'd: 85
  Content with poverty, my Soul, I arm;
  And Vertue, tho' in rags, will keep me warm.

      What is't to me,
Who never sail in her unfaithful Sea,
  If Storms arise, and Clouds grow black;   90
  If the Mast split and threaten wreck?
Then let the greedy Merchant fear
  For his ill gotten gain;
And pray to Gods that will not hear,
While the debating winds and billows bear   95
    His Wealth into the Main.
For me, secure from Fortunes blows,
(Secure of what I cannot lose,)
In my small Pinnace I can sail,
  Contemning all the blustring roar;   100
    And running with a merry gale,
With friendly Stars my safety seek
Within some little winding Creek;
    And see the storm a shore.

To the Pious Memory of the Accomplisht
Young Lady Mrs. Ann Killigrew.
Excellent in the Two Sister-Arts of Poesie,
and Painting. An Ode[1]

THOU youngest Virgin-Daughter of the Skies,
Made in the last Promotion of the *Blest;*
Whose Palms, new pluckt from Paradise,

---

[1] Published in *Poems of Mrs. Anne Killigrew,* 1686. Text of Tonson's edition of
Dryden's *Poems,* 1701.

In spreading *Branches* more sublimely rise,
Rich with Immortal Green above the rest: 5
Whether, adopted to some Neighbouring Star,
Thou rol'st above us, in thy wand'ring Race,
   Or, in Procession fixt and regular,
   Mov'd with the Heav'ns Majestick Pace;
   Or, call'd to more Superiour *Bliss*,   10
Thou tread'st, with Seraphims, the vast *Abyss*.
What ever happy Region is thy place,
Cease thy Celestial Song a little space;
(Thou wilt have time enough for Hymns Divine,
   Since Heav'ns Eternal Year is thine.)   15
Here then a Mortal Muse thy Praise rehearse,
   In no ignoble Verse:
But such as thy own Voice did practise here,
When thy first Fruits of Poesie were giv'n;
To make thy self a welcome Inmate there: 20
   While yet a young Probationer,
   And Candidate of Heav'n.

If by Traduction came thy Mind,
   Our Wonder is the less to find
A Soul so charming from a Stock so good;   25
Thy Father was transfus'd into thy *Blood:*
So wert thou born into a tuneful strain,
(An early, rich, and inexhausted Vein.)
   But if thy Præexisting Soul
   Was form'd, at first, with Myriads more,   30
It did through all the Mighty Poets roul,
   Who *Greek* or *Latine* Laurels wore.
And was that *Sappho* last, which once it was before.
If so, then cease thy flight, *O Heaven-born Mind!*
   Thou hast no *Dross* to purge from thy Rich Ore: 35
   Nor can thy Soul a fairer Mansion find,
   Than was the Beauteous Frame she left behind:
Return, to fill or mend the Quire, of thy Celestial kind.

   May we presume to say, that at thy *Birth*,
New joy was sprung in *Heav'n*, as well as here on *Earth*.   40
   For sure the Milder Planets did combine
   On thy *Auspicious* Horoscope to shine,
   And ev'n the most Malicious were in Trine.
    Thy *Brother-Angels* at thy *Birth*
    Strung each his Lyre, and tun'd it high,   45
    That all the People of the Skie
   Might know a Poetess was born on Earth.
    And then if ever, Mortal Ears
    Had heard the Musick of the Spheres!

And if no clust'ring Swarm of *Bees*   50
On thy sweet Mouth distill'd their golden Dew,
   'Twas that, such vulgar Miracles,
   Heav'n had not Leasure to renew:
For all the *Blest* Fraternity of Love
Solemniz'd there thy *Birth*, and kept thy Holy day above.   55

O gracious God! How far have we
Prophan'd thy Heav'nly Gift of Poesy?
Made prostitute and profligate the Muse,
Debas'd to each obscene and impious use,
Whose Harmony was first ordain'd *Above*   60
For Tongues of *Angels*, and for *Hymns* of *Love*?
O wretched We! why were we hurry'd down
   This lubrique and adult'rate Age,
   (Nay added fat Pollutions of our own)
   T' increase the steaming Ordures of the Stage?   65
What can we say t' excuse our *Second Fall?*
Let this thy *Vestal*, Heaven, attone for all?
Her *Arethusian* Stream remains unsoil'd,
Unmixt with Forreign Filth, and undefil'd,
Her Wit was more than Man, her Innocence a Child!   70

Art she had none, yet wanted none:
   For Nature did that Want supply,
   So rich in Treasures of her Own,
   She might our boasted *Stores* defy: 75
Such Noble Vigour did her Verse adorn,
That it seem'd borrow'd, where 'twas only born.
Her Morals too were in her *Bosom* bred,
   By great Examples daily fed,
What in the best of *Books*, her Father's Life, she read.
And to be read her self she need not fear,   80
Each Test, and ev'ry Light, her Muse will bear,
Though *Epictetus* with his Lamp were there.
Ev'n Love (for Love sometimes her Muse exprest)
Was but a *Lambent-flame* which play'd about her *Breast*:
Light as the Vapours of a Morning Dream,   85
So cold her self, whilst she such Warmth exprest,
'Twas *Cupid* bathing in *Diana*'s Stream.

Born to the Spacious Empire of the *Nine*,
One wou'd have thought, she shou'd have been content
To manage well that Mighty Government;   90
But what can young ambitious Souls confine?
   To the next Realm she stretcht her Sway ⎫
   For *Painture* near adjoyning lay, ⎬
A plenteous Province, and alluring Prey. ⎭

A Chamber of Dependences was fram'd,   **95**
(As Conquerors will never want Pretence,
  When arm'd, to justifie th' Offence)
And the whole Fief, in right of Poetry, she claim'd.
The Country open lay without Defence:
For Poets frequent In-rodes there had made,   **100**
  And perfectly cou'd represent
The Shape, the Face, with ev'ry Lineament;
And all the large Demains which the *Dumb-sister* sway'd,
  All bow'd beneath her Government,
  Receiv'd in Triumph wheresoe're she went.   **105**
Her Pencil drew, what e're her Soul design'd,
And of the *happy Draught* surpass'd the *Image* in her *Mind*.
  The *Sylvan* Scenes of Herds and Flocks,
  And fruitful Plains and barren Rocks,
  Of shallow *Brooks* that flow'd so clear,   **110**
  The bottom did the top appear;
  Of deeper too and ampler Floods,
  Which as in Mirrors, shew'd the Woods;
  Of lofty Trees, with Sacred Shades,
  And Perspectives of pleasant Glades,   **115**
  Where Nymphs of brightest Form appear, ⎫
  And shaggy Satyrs standing near,   ⎬
  Which them at once admire and fear.   ⎭
  The Ruines too of some Majestick Piece,
  Boasting the Pow'r of ancient *Rome* or *Greece*.   **120**
  Whose Statues, Freezes, Columns broken lie,
  And tho' defac'd, the Wonder of the Eye,
  What *Nature, Art*, bold *Fiction* e're durst frame,
  Her forming Hand gave Feature to the Name.
So strange a Concourse ne're was seen before,   **125**
But when the peopl'd *Ark* the whole Creation bore.

  The Scene then chang'd, with bold Erected Look
Our Martial King the sight with Reverence strook:
For not content t' express his Outward Part,
Her Hand call'd out the Image of his Heart,   **130**
His Warlike Mind, his Soul devoid of Fear,   ⎫
His High-designing *Thoughts*, were figur'd there, ⎬
As when, by Magick, Ghosts are made appear. ⎭
  Our Phenix Queen was portrai'd too so bright,
Beauty alone cou'd *Beauty* take so right: **135**
Her Dress, her Shape, her Matchless Grace,
Were all observ'd, as well as Heavenly Face.
With such a Peerless Majesty she stands,
As in that Day she took the Crown from Sacred Hands:
Before a Train of Heroins was seen,   **140**

In *Beauty* foremost, as in Rank, the Queen!
  Thus nothing to her *Genius* was deny'd,
But like a *Ball* of Fire the further thrown,
    Still with a greater *Blaze* she shone,
And her bright Soul broke out on ev'ry side.   145
What next she had design'd, Heaven only knows,
To such Immod'rate Growth her Conquest rose,
That Fate alone its Progress cou'd oppose.

  Now all those Charms, that blooming Grace,
The well-proportion'd Shape, and beauteous Face,   150
Shall never more be seen by Mortal Eyes;
In Earth the much lamented Virgin lies!
  Not Wit, nor Piety cou'd Fate prevent;
  Nor was the cruel *Destiny* content
    To finish all the Murder at a blow,   155
    To sweep at once her *Life*, and *Beauty* too;
But, like a hardn'd Fellon, took a pride
    To work more Mischievously slow,
    And plunder'd first, and then destroy'd.
O double Sacriledge on things Divine,   160
To rob the Relique, and deface the Shrine!
    But thus *Orinda* dy'd:
Heaven, by the same Disease, did both translate,
As equal were their Souls, so equal was their Fate.

  Mean time her *Warlike Brother* on the Seas   165
  His waving Streams to the Winds displays,
And vows for his Return, with vain Devotion, pays,
    Ah, Generous Youth, that Wish forbear,
    The Winds too soon will waft thee here!
Slack all thy Sails, and fear to come,   170
Alas, thou know'st not, thou art wreck'd at home!
No more shalt thou behold thy Sister's Face,
Thou hast already had her last Embrace.
But look aloft, and if thou ken'st from far,
Among the *Pleiad*'s a New-kindl'd Star,   175
If any Sparkles, than the rest, more bright,
'Tis she that shines in that propitious Light.

  When in mid-Air, the Golden Trump shall sound,
    To raise the Nations under Ground;
    When in the Valley of *Jehosaphat*,   180
The Judging God shall close the Book of Fate;
    And there the last *Assizes* keep,
    For those who Wake, and those who Sleep;
    When ratling *Bones* together fly,
From the four Corners of the Skie,   185

When Sinews o're the Skeletons are spread,
Those cloath'd with Flesh, and Life inspires the Dead;
The Sacred Poets first shall hear the Sound,
   And formost from the Tomb shall bound:
For they are cover'd with the lightest Ground,   190
And streight, with in-born Vigour, on the Wing
Like mounting Larks, to the New Morning sing.
There *Thou*, sweet Saint, before the Quire shalt go,
As Harbinger of Heaven, the Way to show,
The Way which thou so well hast learnt below.   195

The Hind and the Panther[1]

Part I

A MILK white *Hind*,[2] immortal and unchang'd,
Fed on the lawns, and in the forest rang'd;
Without unspotted, innocent within,
She fear'd no danger, for she knew no sin.
Yet had she oft been chas'd with horns and hounds,   5
And Scythian shafts; and many winged wounds
Aim'd at Her heart; was often forc'd to fly,
And doom'd to death, though fated not to dy.
   Not so her young; for their unequal line
Was Heroe's make, half humane, half divine.   10
Their earthly mold obnoxious was to fate,
Th' immortal part assum'd immortal state.
Of these a slaughtered army lay in bloud,
Extended o'er the *Caledonian* wood,
Their native walk; whose vocal bloud arose,   15
And cry'd for pardon on their perjur'd foes;
Their fate was fruitful, and the sanguin seed
Endu'd with souls, encreas'd the sacred breed.
So Captive *Israel* multiply'd in chains,
A numerous Exile; and enjoy'd her pains.   20
With grief and gladness mixt, their mother view'd
Her martyr'd offspring, and their race renew'd;
Their corps to perish, but their kind to last,
So much the deathless plant the dying fruit surpass'd.
   Panting and pensive now she rang'd alone,   25
And wander'd in the kingdoms, once Her own.
The common Hunt, though from their rage restrain'd
By sov'reign pow'r, her company disdain'd:

---

[1] Published in April, 1687. Text of the second edition, 1687.
[2] The Roman Catholic Church.

Grin'd as They pass'd, and with a glaring eye
Gave gloomy signs of secret enmity.   30
'Tis true, she bounded by, and trip'd so light
They had not time to take a steady sight.
For truth has such a face and such a meen
As to be lov'd needs only to be seen.
   The bloudy *Bear*[3] an *Independent* beast,   35
Unlick'd to form, in groans her hate express'd.
Among the timorous kind the *Quaking Hare*[4]
Profess'd neutrality, but would not swear.
Next her the *Buffoon Ape*,[5] as Atheists use,
Mimick'd all Sects, and had his own to chuse: 40
Still when the Lyon[6] look'd, his knees he bent,
And pay'd at Church a Courtier's Complement.
   The bristl'd *Baptist Boar*,[7] impure as He,
(But whitn'd with the foam of sanctity)
With fat pollutions fill'd the sacred place,   45
And mountains levell'd in his furious race,
So first rebellion founded was in grace.
But since the mighty ravage which he made
In *German* Forests, had his guilt betrayd,
With broken tusks, and with a borrow'd name   50
He shun'd the vengeance, and conceal'd the shame;
So lurk'd in Sects unseen. With greater guile
False *Reynard*[8] fed on consecrated spoil:
The graceless beast by *Athanasius* first
Was chas'd from *Nice*; then by *Socinus* nurs'd   55
His impious race their blasphemy renew'd,
And natures King through natures opticks view'd.
Revers'd they view'd him lessen'd to their eye,
Nor in an Infant could a God descry:
New swarming Sects to this obliquely tend,   60
Hence they began, and here they all will end.
   What weight of antient witness can prevail
If private reason hold the publick scale?
But, gratious God, how well dost thou provide
For erring judgments an unerring Guide?   65
Thy throne is darkness in th' abyss of light,
A blaze of glory that forbids the sight;
O teach me to believe Thee thus conceal'd,
And search no farther than thy self reveal'd;
But her alone for my Directour take   70

---

[3] The Independents.
[4] The Quakers.
[5] The Freethinkers.
[6] The King of England.
[7] The Anabaptists.
[8] The Arians.

Whom thou hast promis'd never to forsake!
My thoughtless youth was wing'd with vain desires,
My manhood, long misled by wandring fires,
Follow'd false lights; and when their glimps was gone,
My pride struck out new sparkles of her own.   75
Such was I, such by nature still I am,
Be thine the glory, and be mine the shame.
Good life be now my task: my doubts are done,
(What more could fright my faith, than Three in One?)
Can I believe eternal God could lye   ⎫   80
Disguis'd in mortal mold and infancy?   ⎬
That the great maker of the world could dye? ⎭
And after that, trust my imperfect sense
Which calls in question his omnipotence?
Can I my reason to my faith compell,   85
And shall my sight, and touch, and taste rebell?
Superiour faculties are set aside,
Shall their subservient organs be my guide?
Then let the moon usurp the rule of day,
And winking tapers shew the sun his way;   90
For what my senses can themselves perceive
I need no revelation to believe.
Can they who say the Host should be descry'd
By sense, define a body glorify'd?
Impassible, and penetrating parts?   95
Let them declare by what mysterious arts
He shot that body through th' opposing might ⎫
Of bolts and barrs impervious to the light,   ⎬
And stood before his train confess'd in open sight. ⎭
    For since thus wondrously he pass'd, 'tis plain   100
One single place two bodies did contain,
And sure the same Omnipotence as well
Can make one body in more places dwell.
Let reason then at Her own quarry fly,
But how can finite grasp Infinity?   105
    'Tis urg'd again that faith did first commence
By miracles, which are appeals to sense,
And thence concluded that our sense must be
The motive still of credibility.
For latter ages must on former wait,   110
And what began belief, must propagate.
    But winnow well this thought, and you shall find,
'Tis light as chaff that flies before the wind.
Were all those wonders wrought by pow'r divine
As means or ends of some more deep design?   115
Most sure as means, whose end was this alone,
To prove the god-head of th' eternal Son.
God thus asserted: man is to believe

Beyond what sense and reason can conceive.
And for mysterious things of faith rely   120
On the Proponent, heav'ns authority.
If then our faith we for our guide admit,
Vain is the farther search of human wit,
As when the building gains a surer stay,
We take th' unuseful scaffolding away: 125
Reason by sense no more can understand,
The game is play'd into another hand.
Why chuse we then like *Bilanders* to creep }
Along the coast, and land in view to keep,   }
When safely we may launch into the deep?   }   130
In the same vessel which our Saviour bore   }
Himself the Pilot, let us leave the shoar, }
And with a better guide a better world explore. }
Could He his god-head veil with flesh and bloud
And not veil these again to be our food?   135
His grace in both is equal in extent,
The first affords us life, the second nourishment.
And if he can, why all this frantick pain
To construe what his clearest words contain,
And make a riddle what He made so plain?   140
To take up half on trust, and half to try,
Name it not faith, but bungling biggottry.
Both knave and fool the Merchant we may call   }
To pay great summs, and to compound the small. }
For who wou'd break with heav'n, and wou'd not break for all? }
Rest then, my soul, from endless anguish freed;   146
Nor sciences thy guide, nor sense thy creed.
Faith is the best ensurer of thy bliss;
The Bank above must fail before the venture miss.
But heav'n and heav'n-born faith are far from Thee   150
Thou first Apostate to Divinity.
Unkennel'd range in thy *Polonian* Plains;
A fiercer foe th' insatiate *Wolf*[9] remains.
      Too boastful *Britain* please thy self no more,
That beasts of prey are banish'd from thy shoar: 155
The *Bear*, the *Boar*, and every salvage name,
Wild in effect, though in appearance tame,
Lay waste thy woods, destroy thy blissfull bow'r,
And muzl'd though they seem, the mutes devour. }
More haughty than the rest the *wolfish* race, }   160
Appear with belly Gaunt, and famish'd face: }
Never was so deform'd a beast of Grace.
His ragged tail betwixt his leggs he wears   }
Close clap'd for shame, but his rough crest he rears, }
And pricks up his predestinating ears.   }   165

_____
[9] The Presbyterians.

His wild disorder'd walk, his hagger'd eyes,
Did all the bestial citizens surprize.
Though fear'd and hated, yet he rul'd awhile
As Captain or Companion of the spoil.
Full many a year his hatefull head had been   170
For tribute paid, nor since in *Cambria* seen:
The last of all the Litter scap'd by chance,
And from *Geneva* first infested *France*.
Some Authors thus his Pedigree will trace,
But others write him of an upstart Race: 175
Because of *Wickliff*'s Brood no mark he brings
But his innate Antipathy to Kings.
These last deduce him from th' *Helvetian* kind
Who near the *Leman lake* his Consort lin'd.
That fi'ry *Zuynglius* first th' Affection bred,   180
And meagre *Calvin* blest the Nuptial Bed.
In *Israel* some believe him whelp'd long since,
When the proud *Sanhedrim* oppres'd the Prince,
Or, since he will be *Jew*, derive him high'r
When *Corah* with his Brethren did conspire,   185
From *Moyses* Hand the Sov'reign sway to wrest,
And *Aaron* of his Ephod to devest:
Till opening Earth made way for all to pass,
And cou'd not bear the Burd'n of a *class*.
The *Fox* and he came shuffl'd in the Dark,   190
If ever they were stow'd in *Noah's* Ark:
Perhaps not made; for all their barking train
The Dog (a common species) will contain.
And some wild currs, who from their masters ran,
Abhorring the supremacy of man,   195
In woods and caves the rebel-race began.
   O happy pair, how well have you encreas'd,
What ills in Church and State have you redress'd!
With Teeth untry'd, and rudiments of Claws
Your first essay was on your native Laws: 200
Those having torn with Ease, and trampl'd down,
Your Fangs you fasten'd on the miter'd Crown,
And freed from God and Monarchy your Town.
What though your native kennel still be small
Bounded betwixt a Puddle and a Wall,   205
Yet your Victorious Colonies are sent
Where the North Ocean girds the Continent.
Quickned with fire below your Monsters Breed,
In Fenny *Holland* and in fruitful *Tweed*.
And like the first the last effects to be   210
Drawn to the dreggs of a Democracy.
As, where in Fields the fairy rounds are seen,

A rank sow'r herbage rises on the Green;
So, springing where these mid-night Elves advance,
Rebellion Prints the Foot-steps of the Dance. 215
Such are their Doctrines, such contempt they show ⎫
To Heaven above, and to their Prince below, ⎬
As none but Traytors and Blasphemers know. ⎭
God, like the Tyrant of the Skies is plac'd,
And Kings, like slaves, beneath the Croud debas'd. 220
So fulsome is their food, that Flocks refuse
To bite; and only Dogs for Physick use.
As, where the Lightning runs along the Ground,
No husbandry can heal the blasting Wound,
Nor bladed Grass, nor bearded Corn succeeds, 225
But Scales of Scurf, and Putrefaction breeds:
Such Warrs, such Waste, such fiery tracks of Dearth
Their Zeal has left, and such a teemless Earth.
But as the Poisons of the deadliest kind
Are to their own unhappy Coasts confin'd, 230
As only *Indian* Shades of fight deprive,
And Magick Plants will but in *Colchos* thrive;
So Presby'try and Pestilential Zeal
Can only flourish in a Common-weal.
  From *Celtique* Woods is chas'd the *wolfish* Crew, 235
But ah! some Pity e'en to Brutes is due,
Their native Walks, methinks, they might enjoy
Curb'd of their native Malice to destroy.
Of all the Tyrannies on humane kind
The worst is that which Persecutes the mind. 240
Let us but weigh at what offence we strike,
'Tis but because we cannot think alike.
In punishing of this, we overthrow
The Laws of Nations and of Nature too.
Beasts are the Subjects of Tyrannick sway, 245
Where still the stronger on the weaker Prey.
Man only of a softer mold is made;
Not for his Fellows ruine, but their Aid.
Created kind, beneficient and free,
The noble Image of the Deity. 250
One Portion of informing Fire was giv'n
To Brutes, th' Inferiour Family of Heav'n:
The Smith Divine, as with a careless Beat,
Struck out the mute Creation at a Heat:
But when arriv'd at last to humane Race, 255
The Godhead took a deep consid'ring space:
And, to distinguish Man from all the rest,
Unlock'd the sacred Treasures of his Breast:
And Mercy mixt with reason did impart;
One to his Head, the other to his Heart: 260

Reason to Rule, but Mercy to forgive:
The first is Law, the last Prerogative.
And like his Mind his outward form appear'd:
When issuing Naked, to the wondring Herd,
He charm'd their Eyes, and for they lov'd, they fear'd.   265
Not arm'd with horns of arbitrary might,
Or Claws to seize their furry spoils in Fight,
Or with increase of Feet, t'o'ertake 'em in their flight.
Of easie shape, and pliant ev'ry way;
Confessing still the softness of his Clay,   270
And kind as Kings upon their Coronation-Day:
With open Hands, and with extended space
Of Arms to satisfy a large embrace.
Thus kneaded up with Milk, the new made Man
His Kingdom o'er his Kindred world began: 275
Till Knowledge mis-apply'd, mis-understood,
And pride of Empire sour'd his Balmy Blood.
Then, first rebelling, his own stamp he coins;
The Murth'rer *Cain* was latent in his Loins;
And Blood began its first and loudest Cry   280
For diff'ring worship of the Deity.
Thus persecution rose, and farther Space
Produc'd the mighty hunter of his Race.
Not so the blessed *Pan* his flock encreas'd,
Content to fold 'em from the famish'd Beast: 285
Mild were his laws; the Sheep and harmless Hind
Were never of the persecuting kind.
Such pity now the pious Pastor shows,
Such mercy from the *British* Lyon flows,
That both provide protection for their foes.   290
    Oh happy Regions, *Italy* and *Spain*,
Which never did those monsters entertain!
The *Wolfe*, the *Bear*, the *Boar*, can there advance
No native claim of just inheritance.
And self-preserving laws, severe in show,   295
May guard their fences from th' invading foe.
Where birth has plac'd 'em let 'em safely share
The common benefit of vital air.
Themselves unharmful, let them live unharm'd;
Their jaws disabl'd, and their claws disarm'd: 300
Here, only in nocturnal howlings bold,
They dare not seize the Hind nor leap the fold.
More pow'rful, and as vigilant as they,
The *Lyon* awfully forbids the prey.
Their rage repress'd, though pinch'd with famine sore,   305
They stand aloof, and tremble at his roar;
Much is their hunger, but their fear is more.
    These are the chief; to number o'er the rest,

And stand, like *Adam*, naming ev'ry beast,
Were weary work; nor will the Muse describe   310
A slimy-born and sun-begotten Tribe:
Who, far from steeples and their sacred sound,
In fields their sullen conventicles found:
These gross, half animated lumps I leave;
Nor can I think what thoughts they can conceive.   315
But if they think at all, 'tis sure no high'r
Than matter, put in motion, may aspire.
Souls that can scarce ferment their mass of clay; ⎫
So drossy, so divisible are They,   ⎬
As wou'd but serve pure bodies for allay: ⎭   320
Such souls as *Shards* produce, such beetle things,
As only buz to heav'n with ev'ning wings;
Strike in the dark, offending but by chance,
Such are the blind-fold blows of ignorance.
They know not beings, and but hate a name,   325
To them the *Hind* and *Panther* are the same.
   The *Panther*[10] sure the noblest, next the *Hind*,
And fairest creature of the spotted kind;
Oh, could her in-born stains be wash'd away,
She were too good to be a beast of Prey!   330
How can I praise, or blame, and not offend,
Or how divide the frailty from the friend!
Her faults and vertues lye so mix'd, that she
Nor wholly stands condemn'd, nor wholly free.
Then, like her injur'd *Lyon*, let me speak,   335
He cannot bend her, and he would not break.
Unkind already, and estrang'd in part,
The *Wolfe* begins to share her wandring heart.
Though unpolluted yet with actual ill,
She half commits, who sins but in Her will.   340
If, as our dreaming *Platonists* report,
There could be spirits of a middle sort,
Too black for heav'n, and yet too white for hell,
Who just dropt half way down, nor lower fell;
So pois'd, so gently she descends from high,   345
It seems a soft dismission from the skie.
Her house not ancient, whatsoe'er pretence
Her clergy Heraulds make in her defence.
A second century not half-way run
Since the new honours of her blood begun.   350
A *Lyon* old, obscene, and furious made
By lust, compress'd her mother in a shade.
Then, by a left-hand marr'age weds the Dame,
Cov'ring adult'ry with a specious name:

---
[10] The Church of England.

So schism begot; and sacrilege and she,   355
A well-match'd pair, got graceless heresie.
God's and Kings rebels have the same good cause,
To trample down divine and humane laws:
Both wou'd be call'd Reformers, and their hate,
Alike destructive both to Church and State: 360
The fruit proclaims the plant; a lawless Prince ⎫
By luxury reform'd incontinence,   ⎬
By ruins, charity; by riots, abstinence.   ⎭
Confessions, fasts and penance set aside;   ⎫
Oh with what ease we follow such a guide!   ⎬   365
Where souls are starv'd, and senses gratify'd.   ⎭
Where marr'age pleasures, midnight pray'r supply, ⎫
And mattin bells (a melancholly cry)   ⎬
Are tun'd to merrier notes, *encrease* and *multiply*. ⎭
Religion shows a Rosie colour'd face;   ⎫   370
Not hatter'd out with drudging works of grace;   ⎬
A down-hill Reformation rolls apace.   ⎭
What flesh and blood wou'd croud the narrow gate ⎫
Or, till they waste their pamper'd paunches, wait? ⎬
All wou'd be happy at the cheapest rate.   ⎭   375
   Though our lean faith these rigid laws has giv'n,
The full fed *Musulman* goes fat to heav'n;
For his *Arabian* Prophet with delights
Of sense, allur'd his eastern Proselytes.
The jolly *Luther*, reading him, began   380
T'interpret Scriptures by his *Alcoran;*
To grub the thorns beneath our tender feet,
And make the paths of *Paradise* more sweet:
Bethought him of a wife e'er half way gone.
(For 'twas uneasie travailing alone,)   385
And in this masquerade of mirth and love,
Mistook the bliss of heav'n for *Bacchanals* above.
Sure he presum'd of praise, who came to stock
Th' etherial pastures with so fair a flock;
Burnish'd, and bat'ning on their food, to show   390
The diligence of carefull herds below.
   Our *Panther*, though like these she chang'd her head,
Yet, as the mistress of a monarch's bed,
Her front erect with majesty she bore,
The Crozier weilded, and the Miter wore.   395
Her upper part of decent discipline
Shew'd affectation of an ancient line:
And fathers, councils, church and churches head,
Were on her reverend *Phylacteries* read.
But what disgrac'd and disavow'd the rest,   400
Was *Calvin's* brand, that stigmatiz'd the beast.

Thus, like a creature of a double kind,
In her own labyrinth she lives confin'd.
To foreign lands no sounds of Her is come,
Humbly content to be despis'd at home.   405
Such is her faith, where good cannot be had,
At least she leaves the refuse of the bad.
Nice in her choice of ill, though not of best,
And least deform'd, because reform'd the least.
In doubtful points betwixt her diff'ring friends,   410
Where one for substance, one for sign contends,
Their contradicting terms she strives to joyn.
Sign shall be substance, substance shall be sign.
A real presence all her sons allow,
And yet 'tis flat Idolatry to bow,   415
Because the God-head's there they know not how.
Her Novices are taught that bread and wine
Are but the visible and outward sign
Receiv'd by those who in communion joyn.
But th' inward grace, or the thing signify'd,   420
His blood and body, who to save us dy'd;
The faithful this thing signify'd receive.
What is't those faithful then partake or leave?
For what is signify'd and understood,
Is, by her own confession, flesh and blood.   425
Then, by the same acknowledgement, we know
They take the sign, and take the substance too.
The lit'ral sense is hard to flesh and blood,
But nonsense never can be understood.
  Her wild belief on ev'ry wave is tost,   430
But sure no Church can better morals boast.
True to her King her principles are found;
Oh that her practice were but half so sound!
Stedfast in various turns of state she stood,
And seal'd her vow'd affection with her blood;   435
Nor will I meanly tax her constancy,
That int'rest or obligement made the tye,
(Bound to the fate of murdr'd Monarchy:)
(Before the sounding Ax so falls the Vine,
Whose tender branches round the Poplar twine.)   440
She chose her ruin, and resign'd her life,
In death undaunted as an *Indian* wife:
A rare example: But some souls we see
Grow hard, and stiffen with adversity:
Yet these by fortunes favours are undone,   445
Resolv'd into a baser form they run,
And bore the wind, but cannot bear the sun.
Let this be natures frailty or her fate,

Or *Isgrim's*[11] counsel, her new chosen mate;
Still she's the fairest of the fallen Crew,   450
No mother more indulgent but the true.
   Fierce to her foes, yet fears her force to try,
Because she wants innate auctority;
For how can she constrain them to obey
Who has her self cast off the lawful sway?   455
Rebellion equals all, and those who toil
In common theft, will share the common spoil.
Let her produce the title and the right
Against her old superiours first to fight;
If she reform by Text, ev'n that's as plain   460
For her own Rebels to reform again.
As long as words a diff'rent sense will bear,
And each may be his own Interpreter,
Our ai'ry faith will no foundation find:
The word's a weathercock for ev'ry wind: 465
The *Bear*, the *Fox*, the *Wolfe*, by turns prevail,
The most in pow'r supplies the present gale.
The wretched *Panther* crys aloud for aid
To church and councils, whom she first betray'd;
No help from Fathers or traditions train,   470
Those ancient guides she taught us to disdain.
And by that scripture which she once abus'd
To Reformation, stands her self accus'd.
What bills for breach of laws can she prefer,
Expounding which she owns her self may err?   475
And, after all her winding ways are try'd,
If doubts arise she slips herself aside,
And leaves the private conscience for the guide.
If then that conscience set th' offender free,
It bars her claim to church auctority.   480
How can she censure, or what crime pretend,
But Scripture may be constru'd to defend?
Ev'n those whom for rebellion she transmits
To civil pow'r, her doctrine first acquits;
Because no disobedience can ensue,   485
Where no submission to a Judge is due.
Each judging for himself, by her consent,
Whom thus absolv'd she sends to punishment.
Suppose the Magistrate revenge her cause,
'Tis only for transgressing humane laws.   490
How answ'ring to its end a church is made,
Whose pow'r is but to counsel and perswade?
O solid rock, on which secure she stands!

----

[11] The Wolfe.

Eternal house, not built with mortal hands!
O sure defence against th' infernal gate,   495
A patent during pleasure of the state!
  Thus is the *Panther* neither lov'd nor fear'd,
A meer mock Queen of a divided Herd;
Whom soon by lawful pow'r she might controll,
Her self a part submitted to the whole.   500
Then, as the Moon who first receives the light
By which she makes our nether regions bright,
So might she shine, reflecting from afar
The rays she borrow'd from a better Star:
Big with the beams which from her mother flow   505
And reigning o'er the rising tides below:
Now, mixing with a salvage croud, she goes
And meanly flatters her invet'rate foes,
Rul'd while she rules, and losing ev'ry hour
Her wretched remnants of precarious pow'r.   510
  One evening while the cooler shade she sought,
Revolving many a melancholy thought,
Alone she walk'd, and look'd around in vain,
With ruful visage for her vanish'd train:
None of her sylvan subjects made their court;   515
Leveés and coucheés pass'd without resort.
So hardly can Usurpers manage well
Those, whom they first instructed to rebel:
More liberty begets desire of more,
The hunger still encreases with the store.   520
Without respect they brush'd along the wood   ⎫
Each in his clan, and filled with loathsome food;   ⎬
Ask'd no permission to the neighb'ring flood,   ⎭
The *Panther*, full of inward discontent,
Since they wou'd goe, before 'em wisely went: 525
Supplying want of pow'r by drinking first,
As if she gave 'em leave to quench their thirst.
Among the rest, the *Hind*, with fearful face
Beheld from far the common wat'ring place,
Nor durst approach; till with an awful roar   530
The sovereign *Lyon* bad her fear no more.
Encourag'd thus she brought her younglings nigh,
Watching the motions of her Patron's eye,
And drank a sober draught; the rest amaz'd
Stood mutely still, and on the stranger gaz'd: 535
Survey'd her part by part, and sought to find   ⎫
The ten-horn'd monster in the harmless *Hind*,   ⎬
Such as the *Wolfe* and *Panther* had design'd.   ⎭
They thought at first they dream'd, for 'twas offence

With them, to question certitude of sense,   540
Their guide in faith; but nearer when they drew, ⎫
And had the faultless object full in view,   ⎬
Lord, how they all admir'd her heav'nly hiew!   ⎭
Some, who before her fellowship disdain'd,   ⎫
Scarce, and but scarce, from in-born rage restrain'd, ⎬   545
Now frisk'd about her, and old kindred feign'd.   ⎭
Whether for love or int'rest, ev'ry sect
Of all the salvage nation shew'd respect:
The Vice-roy *Panther* could not awe the herd,
The more the company the less they fear'd.   550
The surly *Wolfe* with secret envy burst,   ⎫
Yet cou'd not howl, the *Hind* had seen him first: ⎬
But what he durst not speak, the *Panther* durst. ⎭
   For when the herd suffis'd, did late repair
To ferney heath, and to their forest lare,   555
She made a mannerly excuse to stay,
Proff'ring the *Hind* to wait her half the way:
That since the Skie was clear, an hour of talk
Might help her to beguile the tedious walk.
With much good-will the motion was embrac'd,   560
To chat awhile on their adventures pass'd:
Nor had the grateful *Hind* so soon forgot
Her friend and fellow-suff'rer in the plot.
Yet wondring how of late she grew estrang'd,
Her forehead cloudy, and her count'nance chang'd,   565
She thought this hour th' occasion would present
To learn her secret cause of discontent,
Which, well she hop'd, might be with ease redress'd, ⎫
Consid'ring Her a well-bred civil beast,   ⎬
And more a Gentlewoman than the rest.   ⎭   570
After some common talk what rumours ran,
The Lady of the spotted-muff began.

A Song for St. Cecilia's Day, 1687[1]

FROM Harmony, from Heavenly Harmony
      This Universal Frame began.
   When Nature underneath a heap
      Of jarring Atoms lay,
      And cou'd not heave her Head,   5
   The tuneful Voice was heard from high,
      Arise ye more than dead.

---
[1] Published in 1687. Text of Tonson's edition of Dryden's *Poems*, 1701.

Then cold, and hot, and moist, and dry,
In order to their stations leap,
    And MUSICK's Power obey.   10
From Harmony, from Heavenly Harmony
    This Universal Frame began:
    From Harmony to Harmony
Through all the compass of the Notes it ran,
The Diapason closing full in Man.   15

2.

What Passion cannot MUSICK raise and quell!
    When *Jubal* struck the corded Shell,
  His list'ning Brethren stood around
  And wondring, on their Faces fell
  To worship that Celestial Sound.   20
Less than a God they thought there could not dwell
    Within the hollow of that Shell
    That spoke so sweetly and so well.
What Passion cannot MUSICK raise and quell!

3.

The TRUMPETS loud Clangor,   25
    Excites us to Arms
  With shrill Notes of Anger
  And mortal Alarms,
The double double double beat
  Of the thundring DRUM   30
Cries, heark the Foes come;
Charge, Charge, 'tis too late to retreat.

4.

The soft complaining FLUTE
In dying Notes discovers
The Woes of hopeless Lovers,   35
Whose Dirge is whisper'd by the warbling LUTE.

5.

Sharp VIOLINS proclaim
Their jealous Pangs, and Desperation,
Fury, frantick Indignation,
Depth of Pains, and height of Passion,   40
    For the fair, disdainful Dame.

6.

But oh! what Art can teach
  What human Voice can reach
The sacred ORGANS praise?
Notes inspiring holy Love,   45
Notes that wing their Heavenly ways
  To mend the Choires above.

7.

Orpheus cou'd lead the savage race;
And Trees unrooted left their place;
  Sequacious of the Lyre: 50
But bright *CECILIA* rais'd the wonder high'r;
When to her ORGAN, vocal Breath was giv'n
An Angel heard, and straight appear'd
  Mistaking Earth for Heav'n.

Grand CHORUS

As from the pow'r of Sacred Lays   55
  The Spheres began to Move,
And sung the great Creator's praise
  To all the bless'd above;
So when the last and dreadful hour
This crumbling Pageant shall devour,   60
The TRUMPET *shall be heard on high,*
The Dead shall live, the Living die,
And MUSICK *shall untune the Sky.*

Lines Printed under the Engraved Portrait of Milton, in Tonson's Folio of the "Paradise Lost," 1688[1]

THREE Poets, in three distant Ages born,
Greece, Italy, and *England* did adorn.
The First in loftiness of thought surpass'd,
The Next in Majesty; in both the Last.
The force of Nature could no farther goe;
To make a Third she joynd the former two.

---

[1] Published in Tonson's folio edition of *Paradise Lost*, 1688. Text of first edition.

Mercury's Song to Phædra[1]

FAIR *Iris* I love, and hourly I die,
But not for a lip, nor a languishing Eye:
She's fickle and false, and there we agree;
For I am as false and as fickle as she:
We neither believe what either can say;   5
And, neither believing, we neither betray.

'Tis civil to swear, and say things of course;
We mean not the taking for better for worse.
When present, we love; when absent, agree:
I think not of *Iris*, nor *Iris* of me: 10
The Legend of Love no Couple can find
So easie to part, or so equally join'd.

Song[2]

Enter *Comus* with three Peasants, who sing the following SONG
in Parts.
Com. YOUR Hay it is Mow'd and your Corn is Reap'd;
    Your Barns will be full, and your Hovels heap'd:
    Come, my Boys, Come;
    Come, my Boys, Come;
And merrily Roar out Harvest Home;   5
    Harvest Home,
    Harvest Home;
    And merrily Roar out Harvest Home.
Chorus. Come, my Boys, come, &c.
1 Man. We ha' cheated the Parson, we'll cheat him agen;   10
    For why shou'd a Blockhead ha' One in Ten?
        One in Ten,
        One in Ten;
    For why shou'd a Blockhead ha' One in Ten?
Chorus. One in Ten,   15
        One in Ten;
    For why shou'd a Blockhead ha' One in Ten?
2.   For Prating so long like a Book-learn'd Sot,
    Till Pudding and Dumplin burn to Pot;
        Burn to Pot,   20
        Burn to Pot;

---

[1] Published in *Amphitryon*, 1691, Act IV, Scene i. Text of *Plays*, 1701.
[2] Published in *King Arthur: or, The British Worthy*, 1691, Act V, Scene i. Text
of *Plays*, 1701.

Till Pudding and Dumplin burn to Pot.
Chorus. Burn to Pot, &c.
3. We'll toss off our Ale till we canno' stand,
    And Hoigh for the Honour of Old *England:*   25
        Old *England,*
        Old *England;*
    And Hoigh for the Honour of Old *England.*
Chorus. Old *England,* &c.

The Dance vary'd into a round Country-Dance.

Enter *Venus.*

Venus. Fairest Isle, all Isles Excelling,   30
        Seat of Pleasures, and of Loves;
    Venus, here, will chuse her Dwelling,
        And forsake her *Cyprian* Groves.

    Cupid from his Fav'rite Nation,
        Care and Envy will Remove;   35
    Jealousie, that poysons Passion,
        And Despair that dies for Love.

    Gentle Murmurs, sweet Complaining,
        Sighs that blow the Fire of Love;
    Soft Repulses, kind Disdaining,   40
        Shall be all the Pains you prove.

    Every Swain shall pay his Duty,
        Grateful every Nymph shall prove;
    And as these Excel in Beauty,
        Those shall be Renown'd for Love.   45

Song[1]

No, NO, poor suff'ring Heart no Change endeavour,
Choose to sustain the smart, rather than leave her;
My ravish'd Eyes behold such Charms about her,
I can dye with her, but not live without her.
One tender Sigh of hers to see me Languish,   5
Will more than pay the price of my past Anguish:
Beware, O cruel Fair, how you smile on me,
'Twas a kind Look of yours that has undone me.

Love has in store for me one happy Minute,
And She will end my pain who did begin it;   10

---
[1] Published in *Cleomenes,* 1692, Act II, Scene ii. Text of *Plays,* 1701.

Then no day void of Bliss, or Pleasure leaving,
Ages shall slide away without perceiving:
Cupid shall guard the Door the more to please us,
And keep out Time and Death when they would seize us:
Time and Death shall depart, and say in flying,   15
Love has found out a way to Live by Dying.

Veni Creator Spiritus, Translated in Paraphrase[1]

CREATOR Spirit, by whose aid
The World's Foundations first were laid,
Come visit ev'ry pious Mind;
Come pour thy Joys on Humane Kind:
From Sin, and Sorrow set us free;   5
And make thy Temples worthy Thee.
    O, Source of uncreated Light,
The Father's promis'd *Paraclete!*
Thrice Holy Fount, thrice Holy Fire,
Our Hearts with Heavenly Love inspire;   10
Come, and thy Sacred Unction bring
To Sanctifie us, while we sing!
    Plenteous of Grace, descend from high,
Rich in thy sev'n-fold Energy!
Thou strength of his Almighty Hand,   15
Whose Pow'r does Heaven and Earth Command:
Proceeding, Spirit our Defence, ⎫
Who do'st the Gift of Tongues dispence, ⎬
And crown'st thy Gift, with Eloquence! ⎭
    Refine and purge our Earthy Parts;   20
But, oh, inflame and fire our Hearts!
Our Frailties help, our Vice controul;
Submit the Senses to the Soul;
And when Rebellious they are grown,
Then, lay thy hand, and hold 'em down.   25
    Chace from our Minds the infernal Foe;
And Peace, the fruit of Love, bestow:
And, lest our Feet shou'd step astray,
Protect, and guide us in the way.
    Make us Eternal Truths receive,   30
And practise, all that we believe:
Give us thy self, that we may see

[1] Published in *Examen Poeticum,* 1693. Text of Tonson's edition of Dryden's *Poems,* 1701.

The Father and the Son, by thee.
Immortal Honour, endless Fame
Attend th' Almighty Father's Name: 35
The Saviour Son, be glorify'd,
Who for lost Man's Redemption dy'd:
And equal Adoration be
Eternal *Paraclete*, to thee.

To My Dear Friend Mr. Congreve, On His Comedy, Call'd, The Double-Dealer[1]

WELL then; the promis'd hour is come at last;
The present Age of Wit obscures the past:
Strong were our Syres; and as they Fought they Writ,
Conqu'ring with force of Arms, and dint of Wit;
Theirs was the Gyant Race, before the Flood;   5
And thus, when *Charles* Return'd, our Empire stood.
Like *Janus* he the stubborn Soil manur'd,
With Rules of Husbandry the rankness cur'd:
Tam'd us to manners, when the Stage was rude;
And boistrous *English* Wit, with Art indu'd.   10
Our Age was cultivated thus at length;
But what we gain'd in skill we lost in strength.
Our Builders were, with want of Genius, curst;
The second Temple was not like the first:
Till you, the best *Vitruvius*, come at length;   15
Our Beauties equal; but excel our strength.
Firm *Dorique* Pillars found Your solid Base: ⎫
The Fair *Corinthian* Crowns the higher Space;   ⎬
Thus all below is Strength, and all above is Grace. ⎭
In easie Dialogue is *Fletcher*'s Praise: 20
He mov'd the mind, but had not power to raise.
Great *Johnson* did by strength of Judgment please:
Yet doubling *Fletcher's* Force, he wants his Ease.
In differing Tallents both adorn'd their Age;
One for the Study, t' other for the Stage.   25
But both to *Congreve* justly shall submit,
One match'd in Judgment, both o'er-match'd in Wit.
In him all Beauties of this Age we see;   ⎫
Etherege his Courtship, *Southern's* Purity;   ⎬
The Satire, Wit, and Strength of Manly *Witcherly*. ⎭   30
All this in blooming Youth you have Atchiev'd;
Now are your foil'd Contemporaries griev'd;

---

[1] Published in Congreve's *The Double-Dealer*, 1694. Text of Tonson's edition of Dryden's *Poems*, 1701.

So much the sweetness of your manners move,
We cannot envy you because we Love.
Fabius might joy in *Scipio*, when he saw   35
A Beardless Consul made against the Law,
And joyn his Suffrage to the Votes of *Rome*;
Though He with *Hannibal* was overcome.
Thus old *Romano* bow'd to *Raphel's* Fame;
And Scholar to the Youth he taught, became.   40
  Oh that your Brows my Lawrel had sustain'd,
Well had I been Depos'd, if you had reign'd!
The Father had descended for the Son;
For only You are lineal to the Throne.
Thus when the State one *Edward* did depose;   45
A Greater *Edward* in his room arose.
But now, not I, but Poetry is curs'd;
For *Tom* the second reigns like *Tom* the first.
But let 'em not mistake my Patron's part;
Nor call his Charity their own desert.   50
Yet this I Prophecy; Thou shalt be seen,
(Tho' with some short Parenthesis between:)
High on the Throne of Wit; and seated there,
Not mine (that's little) but thy Lawrel wear.
Thy first attempt an early promise made;   55
That early promise this has more than paid.
So bold, yet so judiciously you dare,
That Your least Praise, is to be Regular.
Time, Place, and Action, may with pains be wrought,
But Genius must be born; and never can be taught.   60
This is your Portion; this Your Native Store;
Heav'n that but once was Prodigal before,
To *Shakespeare* gave as much; she cou'd not give him more.
  Maintain your Post: That's all the Fame You need;
For 'tis impossible you shou'd proceed.   65
Already I am worn with Cares and Age;
And just abandoning th' Ungrateful Stage:
Unprofitably kept at Heav'ns expence,
I live a Rent-charge on his Providence:
But You, whom ev'ry Muse and Grace adorn,   70
Whom I foresee to better Fortune born,
Be kind to my Remains; and oh defend,
Against Your Judgment Your departed Friend!
Let not the Insulting Foe my Fame pursue;
But shade those Lawrels which descend to You: 75
And take for Tribute what these Lines express:
You merit more; nor cou'd my Love do less.

Alexander's Feast;
or, The Power of Musique. An Ode,
in Honour of St. Cecilia's Day[1]

I.

TWAS at the Royal Feast, for *Persia* won,
By *Philip*'s Warlike Son:
Aloft in awful State
The God-like Heroe sate
On his Imperial Throne: 5
His valiant Peers were plac'd around;
Their Brows with Roses and with Myrtles bound.
(So shou'd Desert in Arms be Crown'd:)
The Lovely *Thais* by his side,
Sate like a blooming *Eastern* Bride   10
In Flow'r of Youth and Beauty's Pride.
     Happy, happy, happy Pair!
     None but the Brave
     None but the Brave
     None but the Brave deserves the Fair.   15

CHORUS

Happy, happy, happy Pair!
None but the Brave,
None but the Brave
None but the Brave deserves the Fair.

II.

Timotheus plac'd on high   20
     Amid the tuneful Quire,
     With flying Fingers touch'd the Lyre:
The trembling Notes ascend the Sky,
         And Heav'nly Joys inspire.
The Song began from *Jove*;   25
Who left his blissful Seats above,
(Such is the Pow'r of mighty Love.)
A Dragon's fiery Form bely'd the God:
Sublime on Radiant Spires He rode,
     When He to fair *Olympia* press'd: 30
     And while He sought her snowy Breast:
Then, round her slender Waist he curl'd,
And stamp'd an Image of himself, a Sov'raign of the World.

---

[1] Published in 1697. Text of Tonson's edition of Dryden's *Poems*, 1701.

The list'ning Crowd admire the lofty Sound,
A present Deity, they shout around: 35
A present Deity the vaulted Roofs rebound.
   With ravish'd Ears
   The Monarch hears,
   Assumes the God,
   Affects to nod,   40
  And seems to shake the Spheres.

CHORUS

With ravish'd Ears
The Monarch hears,
Assumes the God,
Affects to nod,   45
And seems to shake the Spheres.

III.

The Praise of *Bacchus* then, the sweet Musician sung;
 Of *Bacchus* ever Fair, and ever Young:
  The jolly God in Triumph comes;
  Sound the Trumpets; beat the Drums;   50
   Flush'd with a purple Grace
   He shews his honest Face,
 Now gives the Hautboys breath; He comes, He comes.
  Bacchus ever Fair and Young,
   Drinking Joys did first ordain: 55
  Bacchus Blessings are a Treasure;
  Drinking is the Soldiers Pleasure;
   Rich the Treasure;
   Sweet the Pleasure;
  Sweet is Pleasure after Pain.   60

CHORUS

Bacchus Blessings are a Treasure;*
Drinking is the Soldier's Pleasure;
Rich the Treasure,
Sweet the Pleasure;
Sweet is Pleasure after Pain.   65

IV.

Sooth'd with the Sound the King grew vain;
 Fought all his Battails o'er again;
And thrice He routed all his Foes; and thrice he slew the slain.
 The Master saw the Madness rise;

His glowing Cheeks, his ardent Eyes; 70
And while He Heav'n and Earth defy'd,
Chang'd his Hand, and check'd his Pride.
He chose a Mournful Muse
Soft Pity to infuse:
He sung *Darius* Great and Good, 75
By too severe a Fate,
Fallen, fallen, fallen, fallen,
Fallen from his high Estate
And weltring in his Blood:
Deserted at his utmost Need, 80
By those his former Bounty fed:
On the bare Earth expos'd He lies,
With not a Friend to close his Eyes.
With down-cast Looks the joyless Victor sate,
Revolving in his alter'd Soul 85
The various Turns of Chance below;
And, now and then, a Sigh he stole;
And Tears began to flow.

CHORUS

Revolving in his alter'd Soul
The various Turns of Chance below; 90
And, now and then, a Sigh he stole;
And Tears began to flow.

V.

The Mighty Master smil'd to see
That Love was in the next Degree:
'Twas but a Kindred-Sound to move; 95
For Pity melts the Mind to Love.
Softly sweet in *Lydian* Measures,
Soon he sooth'd his Soul to Pleasures.
War, he sung, is Toil and Trouble;
Honour but an empty Bubble. 100
Never ending, still beginning,
Fighting still, and still destroying,
If the World be worth thy Winning,
Think, O think, it worth Enjoying.
Lovely *Thais* sits beside thee, 105
Take the Good the Gods provide thee.
The Many rend the Skies, with loud Applause;
So Love was Crown'd, but Musique won the Cause.
The Prince, unable to conceal his Pain,
Gaz'd on the Fair 110
Who caus'd his Care,

And sigh'd and look'd, sigh'd and look'd,
Sigh'd and look'd, and sigh'd again:
At length, with Love and Wine at once oppress'd,
The vanquish'd Victor sunk upon her Breast.   115

CHORUS

The Prince, unable to conceal his Pain,
Gaz'd on the Fair
Who caus'd his Care,
And sigh'd and look'd, sigh'd and look'd,
Sigh'd and look'd, and sigh'd again: 120
At length, with Love and Wine at once oppress'd,
The vanquish'd Victor sunk upon her Breast.

VI.

Now strike the Golden Lyre again;
A lowder yet, and yet a lowder Strain.
Break his Bands of Sleep asunder,   125
And rouze him, like a rattling Peal of Thunder.
Hark, hark, the horrid Sound
Has rais'd up his Head,
As awak'd from the Dead,
And amaz'd, he stares around.   130
Revenge, Revenge, *Timotheus* cries,
See the Furies arise!
See the Snakes that they rear,
How they hiss in their Hair,
And the Sparkles that flash from their Eyes!   135
Behold a ghastly Band,
Each a Torch in his Hand!
Those are *Grecian* Ghosts, that in Battail were slain,
And unbury'd remain
Inglorious on the Plain.   140
Give the Vengeance due
To the Valiant Crew.
Behold how they toss their Torches on high,
How they point to the *Persian* Abodes,
And glitt'ring Temples of their Hostile Gods!   145
The Princes applaud, with a furious Joy;
And the King seiz'd a Flambeau, with Zeal to destroy;
Thais led the Way,
To light him to his Prey,
And, like another *Hellen*, fir'd another *Troy*.   150

CHORUS

And the King seiz'd a Flambeau, with Zeal to destroy;
Thais *led the Way,*
To light him to his Prey,
And, like another Hellen, *fir'd another* Troy.

VII.

Thus, long ago   155
'Ere heaving Bellows learn'd to blow,
While Organs yet were mute;
Timotheus, to his breathing Flute,
And sounding Lyre,
Cou'd swell the Soul to rage, or kindle soft Desire.   160
At last Divine *Cecilia* came,
Inventress of the Vocal Frame;
The sweet Enthusiast, from her Sacred Store,
Enlarg'd the former narrow Bounds,
And added Length to solemn Sounds,   165
With Nature's Mother-Wit, and Arts unknown before,
Let old *Timotheus* yield the Prize,
Or both divide the Crown;
He rais'd a Mortal to the Skies;
She drew an Angel down.   170

GRAND CHORUS

At last, Divine Cecilia *came,*
Inventress of the Vocal Frame;
The sweet Enthusiast, from her Sacred Store,
Enlarg'd the former narrow Bounds,
And added Length to solemn Sounds,   175
With Nature's Mother-Wit, and Arts unknown before.
Let old Timotheus *yield the Prize,*
Or both divide the Crown;
He rais'd a Mortal to the Skies;
She drew an Angel down.   180

SAMUEL BUTLER

(1613-1663-1680)

Hudibras, Part I[1]

The Argument of the First Canto

Sir Hudibras *his passing worth,*
The manner how he sally'd forth:
His Arms and Equipage are shown;
His Horse's Vertues, and his own.
Th' Adventure of the Bear *and* Fiddle,
Is sung, but breaks off in the middle.

Canto I

WHEN *civil* fury first grew high,
And men fell out they knew not why,
When hard *Words, Jealousies,* and *Fears,*
Set Folks together by the Ears,
And made them fight, like mad or drunk,   5
For Dame *Religion* as for Punk,
Whose honesty they all durst swear for,
Though not a man of them knew wherefore:
When *Gospel-Trumpeter* surrounded,
With long-ear'd rout to Battel sounded,   10
And Pulpit, Drum Ecclesiastick,
Was beat with fist, instead of a stick:
Then did Sir *Knight* abandon dwelling,
And out he rode a Colonelling.
  A Wight he was, whose very sight wou'd   15
Entitle him *Mirror of Knighthood;*
That never bent his stubborn knee
To any thing but Chivalry,
Nor put up blow, but that which laid
Right worshipful on Shoulder-blade: 20
Chief of Domestick Knights and Errant,
Either for Chartel or for Warrant:
Great on the Bench, Great in the Saddle,
That could as well bind o'er, as swaddle.
Mighty he was at both of these,   25
And styl'd of *War* as well as *Peace.*
(So some Rats of amphibious nature,

---

[1] Published in 1663. Text of edition of 1678.

Are either for the Land or Water)
But here our Authors make a doubt,
Whether he were more wise, or stout.   30
Some hold the one, and some the other:
But howsoe'er they make a pother,
The difference was so small, his Brain
Outweigh'd his Rage but half a Grain:
Which made some take him for a Tool   35
That Knaves do work with, call'd a Fool.
And offer to lay wagers that
As *Mountaigne* playing with his Cat,
Complains she thought him but an Ass,
Much more she would Sir *Hudibras*.   40
(For that's the Name our valiant Knight
To all his Challenges did write.)
But they're mistaken very much,
'Tis plain enough he was no such.
We grant, although he had much wit,   45
H' was very shie of using it,
As being loath to wear it out,
And therefore bore it not about.
Unless on Holy-days, or so,
As Men their best Apparel do.   50
Beside, 'tis known he could speak *Greek*,
As naturally as Pigs squeek:
That *Latine* was no more difficile,
Than to a Black-bird 'tis to whistle.
Being rich in both, he never scanted   55
His Bounty unto such as wanted;
But much of either would afford,
To many that had not one word.
For *Hebrew* Roots, although th' are found
To flourish most in barren ground,   60
He had such plenty as suffic'd
To make some think him circumcis'd:
And truely so perhaps, he was
'Tis many a Pious Christians case.
    He was in *Logick* a great Critick,   65
Profoundly skill'd in Analytick.
He could distinguish, and divide
A Hair 'twixt *South* and *South-West* side:
On either which he would dispute,
Confute, change hands, and still confute.   70
He'd undertake to prove by force
Of Argument, a Man's no Horse.
He'd prove a Buzard is no Fowl,
And that a *Lord* may be an Owl,
A Calf an *Alderman*, a Goose a *Justice*,   75

And Rooks *Committee-men*, and *Trustees*;
He'd run in Debt by Disputation,
And pay with Ratiocination.
All this by Syllogism, true
In mood and Figure, he would do.   80
For *Rhetorick* he could not ope
His mouth, but out there flew a Trope:
And when he hapned to break off
I' th' middle of his speech, or cough,
H' had hard words, ready to shew why,   85
And tell what Rules he did it by.
Else when with greatest Art he spoke,
You'd think he talk'd like other folk,
For all a Rhetoricians Rules,
Teach nothing but to name his Tools.   90
His ordinary Rate of Speech
In loftiness of sound was rich,
A *Babylonish* dialect,
Which learned Pedants much affect.
It was a parti-colour'd dress   95
Of patch'd and pyball'd Languages:
'Twas English cut on *Greek* and *Latin*,
Like Fustian heretofore on Sattin.
It had an odd promiscuous Tone,
As if h' had talk'd three parts in one.   100
Which made some think when he did gabble,
Th' had heard three Labo'rers of *Babel*;
Or *Cerberus* himself pronounce
A Leash of Languages at once.
This he as volubly would vent   105
As if his stock would ne'er be spent.
And truly to support that charge
He had supplies as vast and large.
For he could coin or counterfeit
New words with little or no wit: 110
Words so debas'd and hard, no stone
Was hard enough to touch them on.
And when with hasty noise he spoke 'em,
The Ignorant for currant took 'em.
That had the Orator who once,   115
Did fill his Mouth with Pibble Stones
When he harangu'd, but known his Phrase,
He would have us'd no other ways.
In *Mathematicks* he was greater
Than *Tycho Brahe*, or *Erra Pater*:   120
For he, by *Geometrick* scale,
Could take the size of *Pots of Ale*;
Resolve by Signs and Tangents streight,

If *Bread* or *Butter* wanted weight;
And wisely tell what hour o' th' day   125
The Clock doth strike, by *Algebra*.
Beside he was a shrewd *Philosopher*,
And had read every Text and gloss over:
What e'er the crabbed'st Author hath
He understood b' implicit Faith,   130
What ever *Sceptick* could inquire for;
For every *why* he had a *wherefore*;
Knew more than forty of them do,
As far as words and terms could go.
All which he understood by Rote,   135
And as occasion serv'd, would quote;
No matter whether right or wrong:
They might be either said or sung.
His Notions fitted things so well,
That which was which he could not tell;   140
But oftentimes mistook th' one
For th' other, as great Clerks have done.
He could reduce all things to Acts,
And knew their Natures by Abstracts,
Where Entity and Quiddity   145
The Ghosts of defunct Bodies flie;
Where Truth in Person does appear,
Like words congeal'd in Northern Air.
He knew *what's what*, and that's as high
As *Metaphysick* Wit can fly,   150
In *School Divinity* as able
As he that hight *Irrefragable*;
Profound in all the Nominal
And real ways beyond them all;
And with as delicate a Hand,   155
Could twist as tough a Rope of Sand.
And weave fine Cobwebs, fit for Skull
That's empty when the Moon is full;
Such as take Lodgings in a Head
That's to be lett unfurnished.   160
He could raise Scruples dark and nice,
And after solve 'em in a trice:
As if Divinity had catch'd
The Itch, of purpose to be scratch'd;
Or, like a Mountebank, did wound   165
And stab her self with doubts profound,
Only to shew with how small pain
The sores of faith are cur'd again;
Although by woful proof we find,
They always leave a Scar behind.   170
He knew the Seat of Paradise,

Could tell in what degree it lies:
And as he was dispos'd, could prove it,
Below the Moon, or else above it.
What *Adam* dreamt of when his Bride 175
Came from her Closet in his side:
Whether the Devil tempted her
By a *High Dutch* Interpreter:
If either of them had a Navel;
Who first made Musick malleable: 180
Whether the Serpent at the fall
Had cloven Feet, or none at all.
All this without a Gloss or Comment,
He would unriddle in a moment:
In proper terms, such as men smatter 185
When they throw out and miss the matter.
For his *Religion* it was fit
To match his Learning and his Wit:
'Twas *Presbyterian* true blew,
For he was of that stubborn Crew 190
Of Errant Saints, whom all men grant
To be the true Church *Militant*:
Such as do build their Faith upon
The holy Text of *Pike* and *Gun*;
Decide all Controversies by 195
Infallible *Artillery*;
And prove their Doctrine Orthodox
By Apostolick *Blows* and *Knocks*;
Call Fire and Sword and Desolation,
A *godly-thorough-Reformation*, 200
Which always must be carry'd on,
And still be doing, never done:
As if Religion were intended
For nothing else but to be mended.
A Sect, whose chief Devotion lies 205
In odd perverse Antipathies;
In falling out with that or this,
And finding somewhat still amiss:
More peevish, cross, and splenetick,
That Dog distract, or Monky sick. 210
That with more care keep Holy-day
The wrong, than others the right way:
Compound for Sins, they are inclin'd to;
By damning those they have no mind to;
Still so perverse and opposite, 215
As if they worshipp'd God for spight,
The self-same thing they will abhor
One way, and long another for.
Free-will they one way disavow,

Another, nothing else allow.   220
All Piety consists therein
In them, in other Men all Sin.
Rather than fail, they will defie
That which they love most tenderly,
Quarrel with *minc'd Pies*, and disparage   225
Their best and dearest friend, *Plum-porridge*;
Fat *Pig* and *Goose* it self oppose,
And blaspheme *Custard* through the *Nose*.
Th' Apostles of this fierce Religion,
Like *Mahomet*'s, were Ass and Widgeon,   230
To whom our Knight, by fast instinct
Of Wit and Temper was so linkt,
As if Hipocrisie and Non-sence
Had got th' Advouson of his Conscience.
  Thus was he gifted and accouter'd,   235
We mean on th' inside, not the outward:
That next of all we shall discuss;
Then listen Sirs, it followeth thus:
  His tawny *Beard* was th' equal grace
Both of his Wisdom and his Face;   240
In Cut and Dy so like a Tile,
A sudden view it would beguile:
The upper part thereof was Whey,
The nether Orange mixt with Grey.
This hairy Meteor did denounce   245
The fall of Scepters and of Crowns;
With grizly type did represent
Declining Age of Government;
And tell with Hieroglyphick Spade,
Its own grave and the State's were made.   250
Like *Sampson*'s Heart-breakers, it grew
In time to make a Nation rue;
Though it contributed its own fall,
To wait upon the publick downfall.
It was Canonick, and did grow   255
In Holy Orders by strict vow;
Of Rule as sullen and severe,
As that of rigid *Cordeliere*:
'Twas bound to suffer Persecution
And Martyrdome with resolution;   260
T' oppose it self against the hate
And vengeance of th' incensed State:
In whose defiance it was worn,
Still ready to be pull'd and torn,
With red-hot Irons to be tortur'd,   265
Revil'd, and spit upon, and martyr'd.
Maugre all which, 'twas to stand fast,

As long as Monarchy should last.
But when the State should hap to reel,
'Twas to submit to fatal Steel,   270
And fall, as it was consecrate
A Sacrifice to fall of State;
Whose thred of life the fatal Sisters
Did twist together with its Whiskers,
And twine so close, that time should never,   275
In life or death, their fortunes sever;
But with his rusty Sickle mow
Both down together at a blow.
   So learned *Taliacotius* from
The brawny part of Porter's Bum,   280
Cut supplemental Noses, which
Would last as long as Parent breech:
But when the Date of *Nock* was out,
Off dropt the Sympathetick Snout.
   His *Back*, or rather Burthen show'd   285
As if it stoop'd with its own load.
For as *Æneas* bore his Sire,
Upon his Shoulders through the Fire:
Our Knight did bear no less a Pack
Of his own Buttocks on his Back: 290
Which now had almost got the Upper-
Hand of his Head, for want of Crupper.
To poize this equally, he bore
A *Paunch* of the same bulk before:
Which still he had a special care   295
To keep well cramm'd with thrifty fare;
As White-pot, Butter-milk, and Curds,
Such as a Countrey house affords;
With other Victual, which anon,
We further shall dilate upon,   300
When of his Hose we come to treat,
The Cub-bord where he kept his meat.
   His *Doublet* was of sturdy Buff,
And though not Sword, yet Cudgel-proof;
Whereby 'twas fitter for his use,   305
That fear'd no blows but such as bruise.
   His *Breeches* were of rugged Woollen,
And had been at the Siege of *Bullen*,
To old King *Harry* so well known,
Some Writers held they were his own.   310
Through they were lin'd with many a piece,
Of Ammunition-Bread and Cheese,
And fat Black-puddings, proper food
For Warriers that delight in Blood;
For, as we said, he always chose   315

To carry Vittle in his Hose.
That often tempted Rats, and Mice,
The Ammunition to surprize:
And when he put a Hand but in
The one or th' other Magazine,   329
They stoutly in defence on't stood
And from the wounded Foe drew bloud,
And till th' were storm'd and beaten out,
Ne'r left the fortifi'd Redoubt;
And though Knights Errant, as some think,   325
Of old did neither eat nor drink,
Because when thorough Desarts vast
And Regions Desolate they past,
Where Belly-timber above ground
Or under was not to be found,   330
Unless they graz'd, there's not one word
Of their Provision, on Record:
Which made some confidently write,
They had no stomachs but to fight,
'Tis false: for *Arthur* wore in Hall   335
Round Table like a Farthingal,
On which, with Shirt pull'd out behind,
And eke before his good Knights din'd.
Though 'twas no Table, some suppose,
But a huge pair of round Trunk-hose;   340
In which he carry'd as much meat
As he and all his Knights could eat;
When laying by their Swords and Truncheons,
They took their Breakfasts, or their Nuncheons;
But let that pass at present, lest   345
We should forget where we digrest;
As learned Authors use, to whom
We leave it, and to th' purpose come,
His Puissant Sword unto his side
Near his undaunted Heart was ty'd,   350
With Basket-hilt, that wou'd hold broth,
And serve for Fight, and Dinner both.
In it he melted Lead for Bullets,
To shoot at Foes, and sometimes Pullets;
To whom he bore so fell a Grutch,   355
He ne'er gave quarter t' any such.
The trenchant blade, *Toledo* trusty,
For want of fighting was grown rusty,
And eat into it self, for lack
Of some body to hew and hack.   360
The peaceful Scabbard where it dwelt,
The Rancor of its Edge had felt:
For of the lower end two handful,

It had devoured 'twas so manful;
And so much scorn'd to lurk in case,   365
As if it durst not shew its face.
In many desperate Attempts
Of Wars, Exigents, Contempts,
It had appear'd with Courage bolder
Than Sergeant *Bum*, invading shoulder.   370
Oft had it ta'en possession,
And Pris'ners too, or made them run.
  This Sword a *Dagger* had his Page.
But was but little for his age:
And therefore waited on him so,   375
As Dwarfs upon Knights Errant do.
It was a serviceable Dudgeon,
Either for fighting or for drudging;
When it had stab'd or broke a head,
It would scrape Trenchers, or chip Bread,   380
Toast Cheese or Bacon, though it were
To bait a Mouse-trap, 'twould not care.
'Twould make clean shooes, and in the Earth
Set Leeks and Onions, and so forth.
It had been Prentice to a Brewer,   385
Where this and more it did endure.
But left the Trade, as many more
Have lately done on the same score.
  In th' Holsters, at his Saddle-bow,
Two aged Pistols he did stow,   390
Among the surplus of such meat
As in his Hose he could not get.
They were upon hard Duty still,
And every night stood Sentinel,
To guard the Magazine i' th' Hose   395
From two legg'd and from four legg'd Foes.
  Thus clad and fortifi'd, Sir Knight
From peaceful home set forth to fight.
But first with nimble active force
He got on th' outside of his *Horse*.   400
For having but one stirrup ty'd
T' his Saddle, on the further side,
It was so short, h' had much adoe
To reach it with his desperate Toe.
But after many strains and heaves   405
He got up to the Saddle eaves.
From whence he vaulted into th' Seat
With so much vigor, strength, and heat,
That he had almost tumbled over
With his own weight, but did recover,   410
By laying hold of Tail and Mane,

Which oft he us'd instead of Reyn.
But now we talk of mounting Steed,
Before we further do proceed,
It doth behove us to say something,　　415
Of that which bore our valiant *Bumkin*.
The Beast was sturdy, large and tall,
With Mouth of Meal and Eyes of Wall:
I would say Eye, for h' had but one,
As most agree, though some say none.　　420
He was well stay'd, and in his Gate
Preserv'd a grave majestick state.
At Spur or Switch no more he skipt,
Or mended pace, than *Spaniard* whipt:
And yet so fiery, he would bound,　　425
As if he griev'd to touch the Ground:
That *Cæsar's* Horse, who, as Fame goes,
Had Corns upon his Feet and Toes,
Was not by half so tender-hooft,
Nor trode upon the ground so soft.　　430
And as that Beast would kneel and stoop,
(Some write) to take his Rider up:
So *Hudibras* his ('tis well known,)
Would often do, to set him down.
We shall not need to say what lack　　435
Of Leather was upon his back:
For that was hidden under pad,
And breech of Knight gall'd full as bad.
His strutting Ribs on both sides show'd
Like furrows he himself had plow'd:　　440
For underneath the skirt of Pannel,
'Twixt every two there was a Channel.
His dragling Tail hung in the Dirt,
Which on his Rider he would flirt
Still as his tender side he prickt,　　445
With arm'd heel or with unarm'd kickt:
For *Hudibras* wore but one Spur,
As wisely knowing, could he stir
To active trot one side of's Horse,
The other would not hang an Arse.　　450
A Squire he had whose name was *Ralph*,
That in th' adventure went his half.
Though Writers (for more statelier tone)
Do call him *Ralpho*, 'tis all one:
And when we can with Meeter safe,　　455
We'll call him so, if not plain *Ralph*,
For Rhime the Rudder is of Verses,
With which like Ships they stear their courses.
An equal stock of Wit and Valour

He had laid in, by birth a Taylor. 460
The mighty *Tyrian* Queen that gain'd
With subtle shreds a Tract of Land,
Did leave it with a Castle fair
To his great Ancestor, her Heir:
From him descended cross-leg'd Knights, 465
Fam'd for their Faith and Warlike Fights
Against the bloudy Caniball,
Whom they destroy'd both great and small.
This sturdy Squire had as well
As the bold *Trojan* Knight, seen hell, 470
Not with a counterfeited Pass
Of Golden Bough, but true Gold-lace.
His knowledge was not far behind
The Knights, but of another kind,
And he another way came by't, 475
Some call it *Gift*, and some *New light*;
A liberal Art, that costs no pains
Of Study, Industry, or Brains.
His Wits were sent him for a Token,
But in the Carriage crackt and broken 480
Like Commendation Nine-pence, crookt
With to and from my Love, it lookt,
He ne'r consider'd it, as loath
To look a Gift-horse in the Mouth;
And very wisely would lay forth 485
No more upon it than 'twas worth.
But as he got it freely, so
He spent it frank and freely too.
For Saints themselves will sometimes be,
Of Gifts that cost them nothing, free. 490
By means of this, with *hem* and *cough*,
Prolongers to enlightned Snuff,
He could deep Mysteries unriddle,
As easily as thread a Needle;
For as of Vagabonds we say, 495
That they are ne'r beside their way:
What e'r men speak by this *New Light*,
Still they are sure to be i' th' right.
'Tis a *Dark-Lanthorn* of the Spirit,
Which none see by but those that bear it. 500
A Light that falls down from on high,
For Spiritual Trades to couzen by:
An *Ignis Fatuus* that bewitches,
And leads Men into Pools and Ditches,
To make them *dip* themselves, and sound 505
For Christendom and dirty Pond;
To dive like Wild-foul for Salvation,

And fish to catch Regeneration.
This Light inspires, and plays upon
The nose of Saint like Bag-pipe drone,   510
And speaks through hollow empty Soul,
As through a Trunk, or whisp'ring hole,
Such language as no mortal Ear
But spiritual Eve-droppers can hear.
So *Phœbus* or some friendly Muse   515
Into small Poets song infuse;
Which they at second-hand reherse
Through Reed or Bag-pipe, Verse for Verse.
  Thus *Ralph* became infallible,
As three or four-leg'd Oracle,   520
The ancient Cup, or modern Chair,
Spoke truth point-blank, though unaware:
  For mystick Learning, wondrous able
In Magick *Talisman*, and *Cabal*,
Whose Primitive Tradition reaches   525
As far as *Adam*'s first green Breeches:
Deep-sighted in Intelligences,
Idea's, Atomes, Influences;
And much of *Terra Incognita*,
Th' intelligible World could say;   530
A deep occult Philosopher,
As learn'd as the *Wild Irish* are,
Or Sir *Agrippa*, for profound
And solid Lying much renown'd:
He *Anthroposophus*, and *Floud*,   535
And *Jacob Behmen* understood;
Knew many an Amulet and Charm,
That would do neither good nor harm:
In *Rosy-Crucian* Lore as Learned,
As he that *Veré adeptus* earned.   540
He understood the speech of Birds
As well as they themselves do words:
Could tell what subtlest *Parrots* mean,
That speak and think contrary clean;
What *Member* 'tis of whom they talk   545
When they cry *Rope*, and *Walk Knave, walk*.
He'd extract numbers out of matter,
And keep them in a Glass, like water,
Of Sov'raign pow'r to make men wise;
For dropt in blere, thick-sighted Eyes,   550
They'd make them see in darkest night,
Like Owls, though pur-blind in the light.
By help of these (as he profest)
He had *First Matter* seen undrest:
He took her naked all alone,   555

Before one Rag of *Form* was on.
The *Chaos* too he had descry'd,
And seen quite through, or else he ly'd:
Not that of Past-board which men shew
For Goats at Fair of *Barthol'mew;*   560
But its great Gransire, first o' th' name,
Whence that and *Reformation* came:
Both Cousin-Germans, and right able
T' inveigle and draw in the Rabble.
But *Reformation* was, some say,   565
O' th' younger house to *Puppet-Play.*
He could foretell whats'ever was
By consequence to come to pass.
As Death of Great Men, Alterations,
Diseases, Battels, Inundations.   570
All this without th' Eclipse of Sun,
Or dreadful Comet, he hath done
By inward Light, a way as good,
And easie to be understood.
But with more lucky hit than those   575
That use to make the Stars depose,
Like Knights o' th' Post, and falsly charge
Upon themselves what others forge:
As if they were consenting to
All mischief in the World men do: 580
Or like the Dev'l, did tempt and sway 'em
To Rogueries, and then betray 'em.
They'l search a Planet's house, to know,
Who broke and robb'd a house below:
Examine *Venus*, and the *Moon*   585
Who stole a Thimble and a Spoon:
And though they nothing will confess,
Yet by their very looks can guess,
And tell what guilty Aspect bodes,
Who stole, and who receiv'd the Goods.   590
They'l question *Mars*, and by his look
Detect who 'twas that nimm'd a Cloke:
Make *Mercury* confess and peach
Those Thieves which he himself did teach.
They'l find i' th' Phisiognomies   595
O' th' Planets all mens destinies.
Like him that took the Doctor's Bill,
And swallow'd it instead o' th' Pill.
Cast the Nativity o' th' Question,
And from Positions to be guest on,   600
As sure as if they knew the Moment
Of Natives birth, tell what will come on 't.
They'l feel the Pulses of the Stars,

To find out Agues, Coughs, Catarrhs;
And tell what *Crysis* does divine
The Rot in Sheep, or Mange in Swine:
In Men what gives or cures the Itch,
What makes them Cuckolds, poor or rich:
What gains or loses, hangs or saves;
What makes men great, what fools or knaves;
But not what wise, for only of those
The Stars (they say) cannot dispose,
No more than can the Astrologians.
There they say right, and like true *Trojans*.
This *Ralpho* knew, and therefore took
The other course, of which we spoke.
Thus was th' accomplish'd Squire endu'd
With Gifts and Knowledge, per'lous shrew'd.
Never did trusty Squire with Knight,
Or Knight with Squire jump more right.
Their Arms and Equipage did fit,
As well as Virtues, Parts, and Wit.
Their Valors too were of a Rate,
And out they sally'd at the Gate.
Few miles on horseback had they jogged,
But fortune unto them turn'd dogged.
For they a sad adventure met,
Of which we now prepare to Treat:
But e'er we venture to unfold
Atchievements so resolv'd and bold,
We should as learned Poets use,
Invoke the assistance of some *Muse*;
However Criticks count it sillier
Than Juglers talking t' a Familiar.
We think 'tis no great matter which,
They're all alike, yet we shall pitch
On one that fits our purpose most,
Whom therefore thus do we accost.
Thou that with Ale or viler Liquors,
Didst inspire *Withers*, *Prin*, and *Vickars*,
And force them, though it were in spight
Of Nature, and their Stars, to write;
Who, as we finde in sullen Writs,
And cross-graind Works of modern Wits,
With Vanity, Opinion, Want,
The wonder of the Ignorant,
The Praises of the Author, penn'd
By himself, or wit-ensuring friend,
The Itch of Picture in the Front,
With Bays, and wicked Rhime upon 't,
All that is left o' th' forked Hill

To make men scribble without skill,
Canst make a Poet, spight of fate,
And teach all People to translate;
Though out of Languages in which   655
They understand no Part of Speech:
Assist me but this once, I'mplore,
And I shall trouble thee no more.
In Western Clime there is a Town
To those that dwell therein well known;   660
Therefore there needs no more be sed here
We unto them refer our Reader:
For brevity is very good,
When w'are, or are not understood.
To this Town People did repair   665
On days of Market or of Fair,
And to crack'd Fiddle, and hoarse Tabor
In merriment did drudge and labor:
But now a sport more formidable
Had rak'd together Village rabble.   670
'Twas an old way of Recreating,
Which learned Butchers call *Bear-baiting*:
A bold advent'rous exercise,
With ancient *Heroe's* in high prize;
For Authors do affirm it came   675
From *Istmian* or *Nemean* game;
Others derive it from the *Bear*
That's fixt in Northern Hemisphere,
And round about the Pole does make
A circle like a Bear at stake,   680
That at the Chain's end wheels about,
And over-turns the Rabble-rout.
For after solemn Proclamation
In the Bear's name (as is the fashion,
According to the Law of Arms,   685
To keep men from inglorious harms)
That none presume to come so near
As forty foot of stake of Bear;
If any yet be so fool-hardy,
T'expose themselves to vain Jeopardy;   690
If they come wounded off and lame
No honour's got by such a maim.
Although the Bear gain'd much b'ing bound
In honour to make good his ground.
When he's engag'd, and take no notice,   695
If any press upon him, who 'tis,
But let them know at their own cost
That he intends to keep his post.
This to prevent, and other harms,

Which always wait on feats of Arms,   700
(For in the hurry of a Fray
'Tis hard to keep out of harm's way)
Thither the Knight his course did stear,
To keep the peace 'twixt *Dog* and *Bear*;
As he believ'd h' was bound to doe,   705
In Conscience and Commission too.
And therefore thus bespoke the Squire;
  We that are wisely mounted higher
Then Constables, in Curule wit,
When on Tribunal bench we sit,   710
Like Speculators, should foresee
From *Pharos* of Authority,
Portended Mischiefs farther then
Low Proletarian Tithing-men.
And therefore being inform'd by bruit,   715
That *Dog* and *Bear* are to dispute;
For so of late men fighting name,
Because they often prove the same;
(For where the first does hap to be
The last does *coincidere*)   720
Quantum in nobis, have thought good,
To save th' expence of Christian blood,
And try if we by Mediation
Of Treaty and accommodation
Can end the quarrel, and compose   725
The bloudy Duel without blows.
Are not our Liberties, our Lives,
The Laws, Religion, and our Wives
Enough at once to lie at stake,
For *Cov'nant* and the *Causes* sake;   730
But in that quarrel *Dogs* and *Bears*
As well as we must venture theirs?
This Feud by *Jesuits* invented,
By *evil Counsel* is fomented,
There is a *Machiavilian* Plot,   735
(Though ev'ry *Nare olfact* it not)
A deep design in 't to divide
The well-affected that confide,
By setting Brother against Brother,
To claw and curry one another.   740
Have we not enemies *plus satis*,
That *Cane & angue pejus* hate us?
And shall we turn our fangs and claws
Upon our selves without a cause?
That some occult design doth lie   745
In bloudy *Cynarctomachy*
Is plain enough to him that knows

How Saints lead Brothers by the Nose.
I wish my self a Pseudo-Prophet,
But sure some mischief will come of it: 750
Unless by providential wit
Or force we averruncate it.
For what design, what interest
Can Beast have to encounter Beast?
They fight for no espoused *Cause*; 755
Frail *Priviledge*, *Fundamental Laws*,
Nor for a *through Reformation*,
Nor *Covenant*, nor *Protestation*;
Nor *Liberty of Consciences*,
Nor Lords and Commons *Ordinances*; 760
Nor for the *Church*, nor for *Church Lands*,
To get them in their own no Hands;
Nor *evil Counsellors* to bring
To Justice that seduce the King;
Nor for the worship of us men, 765
Though we have done as much for them.
Th' *Egyptians* worshipp'd *Dogs*, and for
Their faith made fierce and zealous Warr.
Others ador'd a *Rat*, and some
For that Church suffer'd Martyrdome. 770
The *Indians* fought for the truth
Of th' *Elephant*, and *Monkey*'s Tooth:
And many, to defend that faith,
Fought it out *mordicus* to death.
But no Beast ever was so slight, 775
For Man, as for his God, to fight.
They have more wit, alas! and know
Themselves and us better than so.
But we, we onely do infuse
The Rage in them like *Boute-feus*. 780
'Tis our example that instills
In them th' infection of our ills.
For as some late Philosophers
Have well observed, Beasts that converse
With Man, take after him, as Hogs 785
Get Pigs all th' year, and Bitches Dogs.
Just so by our example Cattle
Learn to give one another Battel.
We read in *Nero*'s time, the Heathen,
When they destroy'd the *Christian Brethren*, 790
They sow'd them in the skins of Bears,
And then set Dogs about their Ears:
From whence, no doubt, th' invention came
Of this lewd Antichristian Game.
　　To this, quoth *Ralpho*, Verily, 795

The Point seems very plain to be.
It is an Antichristian Game,
Unlawful both in thing and name;
First for the *Name*, The word *Bear-baiting*,
Is Carnal, and of man's creating: 800
For certainly there's no such word
In all the *Scripture* on Record.
Therefore unlawful and a sin,
And so is (secondly) the *thing*.
A vile *Assembly* 'tis, that can   805
No more be prov'd by Scripture than
Provincial, Classick, National;
Mere humane Creature-Cobwebs all.
Thirdly, it is Idolatrous:
For when men run a-whoring thus   810
With their Inventions whatsoe'r
The thing be, whether *Dog* or *Bear,*
It is Idolatrous and *Pagan*
No less than worshipping of *Dagon*.
   Quoth *Hudibras*, I smell a *Rat*;   815
Ralpho, thou dost prevaricate.
For though the *Thesis* which thou lay'st
Be true *ad amussim* as thou say'st:
(For that *Bear-baiting* should appear
Jure Divino lawfuller   820
Than *Synods* are, thou dost deny,
Totidem verbis so do I)
Yet there's a fallacy in this:
For if by sly *Homæosis*,
Thou would'st Sophistically imply   825
Both are unlawful, I deny.
   And I (quoth *Ralpho*) do not doubt
But *Bear-baiting* may be made out
In Gospel-times, as lawful as is
Provincial or *Parochial Classis*:   830
And that both are so near of kin,
And like in all as well as sin,
That put them in a bag and shake 'em,
Your self o' th' sudden would mistake 'em,
And not know which is which, unless   835
You measure by their wickedness:
For 'tis not hard t' imagine whether
O' th' two is worst, though I name neither.
   Quoth *Hudibras*, thou offer'st much,
But art not able to keep touch.   840
Mira de lente, as 'tis i' th' Adage,
Id est, to make a Leak a Cabbage.
Thou canst at best but overstrain

A Paradox, and th' own hot brain:
For what can *Synods* have at all 845
With *Bears* that's Analogical?
Or what relation has debating
Of Church-Affairs with *Bear-baiting?*
A just comparison still is,
Of things *ejusdem generis*. 850
And then what *Genus* rightly doth,
Include and comprehend them both?
If *Animal*, both of us may
As justly pass for *Bears* as they.
For we are Animals no less, 855
Although of different *Specieses*.
But, *Ralpho* this is no fit place,
Nor time to argue out the Case:
For now the Field is not far off,
Where we must give the world a proof 860
Of Deeds, not Words, and such as suit
Another manner of Dispute.
A Controversie that affords
Actions for Arguments, not Words:
Which we must manage at a rate 865
Of Prowess and Conduct adæquate;
To what our place and fame doth promise,
And all the godly expect from us.
Nor shall they be deceiv'd, unless
W' are slurr'd and outed by success: 870
Success, the Mark no mortal Wit,
Or surest hand can always hit:
For whatsoe're we perpetrate,
We do but row, we 'are steer'd by *Fate*,
Which in success oft disinherits, 875
For spurious Causes, noblest merits.
Great Actions are not always true Sons
Of great and mighty Resolutions:
Nor doth the bold'st attempts bring forth
Events still equal to their worth; 880
But sometimes fail, and in their stead,
Fortune and Cowardice succeed,
Yet we have no great cause to doubt,
Our actions still have born us out.
Which though th' are known to be so ample, 885
We need no copy from example,
We' are not the onely person durst
Attempt this Province, nor the first.
In Northern Clime a valorous Knight
Did whilom kill his Bear in fight, 890

And wound a Fidler: we have both
Of these the objects of our Wroth,
And equal Fame and Glory from
Th' Attempt or Victory to come.
'Tis sung, There is a valiant *Marmaluke*   895
In foreign Land, yclep'd ——²
To whom we have been oft compar'd
For Person, Parts, Address and Beard:
Both equally reputed stout,
And in the same Cause both have fought.   900
He oft in such Attempts as these
Came off with glory and success.
Nor will we fail in th' execution,
For want of equal Resolution.
Honour is, like a Widow, won   905
With brisk Attempt and putting on;
With ent'ring manfully, and urging;
Not slow approaches, like a Virgin.
  This said, as once the *Phrygian* Knight,
So ours, with rusty steell, did smite   910
His *Trojan* Horse, and just as much
He mended pace upon the touch;
But from his empty stomach groan'd
Just as that hollow Beast did sound,
And angry answer'd from behind,   915
With brandish'd Tail and blast of Wind.
So have I seen with armed heel,
A Wight bestride a *Commonweal*;
Whil'st still the more he kick'd and spurr'd,
The less the sullen Jade has stirr'd.   920

SIR CHARLES SEDLEY

(1639?-1663-1701)

To Cloris¹

CLORIS, I cannot say your Eyes
Did my unwary Heart surprize;
Nor will I swear it was your Face,

---

² Sir Samuel Luke.
¹ Published in *A Collection of Poems, Written upon Several Occasions*, 1672. Text of *Poetical Works*, ed. Ayloffe, 1707.

Your Shape, or any nameless Grace:
For you are so intirely Fair,   5
To love a Part, Injustice were;
No drowning Man can know which Drop
Of Water his last Breath did stop;
So when the Stars in Heaven appear,
And joyn to make the Night look clear;   10
The Light we no one's Bounty call,
But the obliging Gift of all.
He that does Lips or Hands adore,
Deserves them only, and no more;
But I love All, and every Part,   15
And nothing less can ease my Heart.
Cupid, that Lover, weakly strikes,
Who can express what 'tis he likes.

Song[1]

Love still has something of the Sea,
    From whence his Mother rose;
No time his Slaves from Doubt can free,
    Nor give their Thoughts repose:

They are becalm'd in clearest Days,   5
    And in rough Weather tost;
They wither under cold Delays,
    Or are in Tempests lost.

One while they seem to touch the Port,
    Then straight into the Main,   10
Some angry Wind in cruel sport
    The Vessel drives again.

At first Disdain and Pride they fear,
    Which if they chance to 'scape,
Rivals and Falshood soon appear   15
    In a more dreadful shape.

By such Degrees to Joy they come,
    And are so long withstood,
So slowly they receive the Sum,
    It hardly does them good.   20

---

[1] Published in *A Collection of Poems, Written upon Several Occasions*, 1672. Text of *Poetical Works*, ed. Ayloffe, 1707.

'Tis cruel to prolong a Pain,
    And to defer a Joy;
Believe me, gentle *Celemene*
    Offends the winged Boy.

An hundred thousand Oaths your Fears   25
    Perhaps would not remove;
And if I gaz'd a thousand Years
    I could no deeper love.

The Indifference[1]

THANKS, fair *Urania*; to your Scorn
I now am free, as I was born,
Of all the Pain that I endur'd
By your late Coldness I am cur'd.

In losing me, proud Nymph, you lose   5
The humblest Slave your Beauty Knows;
In losing you, I but throw down
A cruel Tyrant from her Throne.

My ranging Love did never find
Such Charms of Person and of Mind;   10
Y'ave Beauty, Wit, and all things know,
But where you shou'd your Love bestow.

I unawares my Freedom gave,
And to those Tyrants grew a Slave;
Would you have kept what you had won,   15
You should have more Compassion shewn.

Love is a Burthen, which two Hearts,
When equally they bear their Parts,
With Pleasure carry; but no one,
Alas, can bear it long alone.   20

I'm not of those who court their Pain,
And make an Idol of Disdain;
My Hope in Love does ne'er expire,
But it extinguishes Desire.

¹ Published in *A Collection of Poems, Written upon Several Occasions*, 1672. Text of *Poetical Works*, ed. Ayloffe, 1707.

Nor yet of those who ill receiv'd,   25
Wou'd have it otherwise believ'd
And, where their Love cou'd not prevail,
Take the vain Liberty to rail.

Whoe'er wou'd make his Victor less,
Must his own weak Defence confess,   30
And while her Power he does defame,
He poorly doubles his own Shame.

Even that Malice does betray,
And speak Concern another way;
And all such Scorn in Men is but   35
The Smoke of Fires ill put out.

He's still in Torment, whom the Rage
To Detraction does engage;
In Love Indifference is sure
The only sign of perfect Cure.   40

Advice to the Old Beaux[1]

SCRAPE no more your harmless Chins,
    Old Beaux, in hope to please;
You shou'd repent your former Sins,
    Not study their Increase;
Young awkard Fops, may shock our Sight,   5
But you offend by Day and Night.

In vain the Coachman turns about,
    And whips the dappl'd Greys;
When the old Ogler looks out,
    We turn away our Face.   10
True Love and Youth will ever charm,
But both affected, cannot warm.

Summer-fruits we highly prize,
    They kindly cool the Blood;
But Winter berries we despise,   15
    And leave 'em in the Wood;
On the Bush they may look well,
But gather'd, lose both taste and smell.

---

[1] Published in the *Gentleman's Journal*, August, 1693. Text of *Poetical Works*, ed. Ayloffe, 1707.

That you languish, that you dye,
    Alas, is but too true;
Yet tax not us with Cruelty,
    Who daily pity you.
Nature henceforth alone accuse,
In vain we grant, if she refuse.   20

Song[1]

SMOOTH was the Water, calm the Air,
    The Evening-Sun deprest,
Lawyers dismist the noisie Bar,
    The Labourer at rest,

When *Strephon*, with his charming Fair,   5
    Cross'd the proud River *Thames*,
And to a Garden did repair,
    To quench their mutual Flames.

The crafty Waiter soon espy'd
    Youth sparkling in her Eyes;   10
He brought no Ham, nor Neats-tongues dry'd,
    But Cream and Strawberries.

The amorous *Strephon* ask'd the Maid,
    What's whiter than this Cream?
She blush'd, and could not tell, she said: 15
    Thy Teeth, my pretty Lamb.

What's redder than these Berries are?
    I know not, she reply'd:
Those lips, which I'll no longer spare,
    The burning Shepherd cry'd.   20

And strait began to hug her:
    This Kiss, my Dear,
Is sweater far
    Than Strawberries, Cream and Sugar.

---

[1] Published in *Miscellaneous Works,* ed. Ayloffe, 1702. Text of 1707 edition.

Song[1]

Phillis is my only Joy,
  Faithless as the Winds or Seas;
Sometimes coming, sometimes coy,
  Yet she never fails to please;
    If with a Frown   5
    I am cast down,
    Phillis smiling,
    And beguiling,
Makes me happier than before.

Tho', alas, too late I find,   10
  Nothing can her Fancy fix;
Yet the Moment she is kind,
  I forgive her all her Tricks;
    Which, tho' I see,
    I can't get free;   15
    She deceiving,
    I believing;
What need Lovers wish for more?

Sir George Etherege

(1635?-1664-1691)

Song[2]

If she be not as kind as fair,
  But peevish and unhandy,
Leave her, she's only worth the Care
  Of some spruce Jack-a-dandy.
I wou'd not have thee such an Ass,   5
Hadst thou ne're so much leisure,
To sign and whine for such a Lass
  Whose Pride's above her Pleasure.

---

[1] Published in *Miscellaneous Works*, ed. Ayloffe, 1702. Text of 1707 edition.
[2] Published in *Love in a Tub*, 1664, Act II, Scene iii. Text of *Works*, 1704.

To a Lady, Asking Him How Long He would Love Her[1]

IT IS not, *Celia*, in our Power
To say how long our Love will last;
It may be we, within this Hour,
May lose those Joys we now do taste:
The Blessed, that immortal be,   5
From Change in Love are only free.

Then, since we mortal Lovers are,
Ask not how long our Love will last;
But while it does, let us take care
Each Minute be with Pleasure past: 10
Were it not Madness to deny
To live, because w' are sure to die?

Song[2]

THE Pleasures of Love, and the Joys of good Wine,
To perfect our Happiness wisely we join.
We to Beauty all Day
Give the Soveraign Sway,
And her Favourite Nymphs devoutly obey.   5
At the Plays we are constantly making our Court,
And when they are ended we follow the Sport.
To the Mail and the Park,
Where we love 'till 'tis dark;
Then sparkling Champaign   10
Puts an end to their Reign;
It quickly recovers
Poor languishing Lovers,
Make us frolick and gay, and drowns all our Sorrow.
But alas! we relapse again on the Morrow.   15
Let ev'ry Man stand
With his Glass in his Hand,
And briskly discharge at the Word of Command.
Here's a Health to all those
Whom to Night we depose.   20
Wine and Beauty by turns great Souls should inspire.
Present all together, and now Boys give Fire——

---

[1] Published in 1673. Text of *A Collection of Poems*, third edition, 1716.
[2] Published in *The Man of Mode; or, Sir Fopling Flutter*, 1676, Act IV, Scene i. Text of *Works*, 1704.

To a Very Young Lady[1]

SWEETEST Bud of Beauty, may
No untimely Frost decay
Th' early Glories which we trace,
Blooming in thy matchless Face;
But kindly opening, like the Rose,   5
Fresh Beauties every day disclose,
Such as by Nature are not shown
In all the Blossoms she has blown.
And then what Conquest shall you make,
Who Hearts already daily take?   10
Scorch'd in the Morning with thy Beams,
How shall we bear those sad Extremes,
Which must attend thy threatning Eyes,
When thou shalt to thy Noon arise?

CHARLES COTTON

(1630-1670-1687)

The Retirement
Stanzas Irreguliers to Mr. Izaak Walton[2]

FAREWELL thou busie World, and may
        We never meet again:
Here I can eat, and sleep, and pray,
And doe more good in one short day,
Than he who his whole Age out-wears   5
Upon thy most conspicuous Theatres,
Where nought but Vice and Vanity do reign.

Good God! how sweet are all things here!
How beautifull the Fields appear!
How cleanly do we feed and lie!   10
Lord! what good hours do we keep!
        How quietly we sleep!

---

[1] Published in *A Collection of Poems*, 1701. Text of third edition, 1716.
[2] Published in *The Compleat Angler*, Part II, 1676. Text of *Poems on Several Occasions*, 1689.

What Peace! what Unanimity!
How innocent from the leud Fashion,
Is all our bus'ness, all our Conversation!   15

Oh how happy here's our leisure!
Oh how innocent our pleasure!
Oh ye Vallies, oh ye Mountains,
Oh ye Groves and Chrystall Fountains,
    How I love at liberty,   20
    By turn to come and visit ye!

O Solitude, the Soul's best Friend,
That man acquainted with himself dost make,
And all his Maker's Wonders to intend;
    With thee I here converse at will,   25
    And would be glad to do so still;
For it is thou alone that keep'st the Soul awake.

How calm and quiet a delight
        It is alone
To read, and meditate, and write,   30
By none offended, nor offending none;
To walk, ride, sit, or sleep at one's own ease,
And pleasing a man's self, none other to displease!

Oh my beloved Nymph! fair Dove,
Princess of Rivers, how I love   35
    Upon thy flow'ry Banks to lie,
    And view thy Silver stream,
When gilded by a Summer's Beam,
And in it all thy wanton Fry
        Playing at liberty,   40
    And with my Angle upon them,
        The All of Treachery
I ever learn'd to practise and to try!

Such streams *Rome*'s yellow *Tiber* cannot show,
Th' *Iberian Tagus*, nor *Ligurian Po;*   45
    The *Meuse*, the *Danube*, and the *Rhine*,
    Are puddle-water all compar'd with thine;
And *Loire*'s pure streams yet too polluted are
    With thine much purer to compare:
The rapid *Garonne*, and the winding *Seine*   50
        Are both too mean,
    Beloved Dove, with thee
        To vie Priority:
Nay, *Tame* and *Isis*, when conjoyn'd, submit,
And lay their Trophies at thy Silver Feet.   55